Praise for *Leadership Lessons from a UPS Driver*

"UPSers believe in the principle that your mission throughout your career is to leave the company in a better state than when you arrived. Ron Wallace did that at UPS. If you follow Ron's leadership insights in this book, you too will leave your company in a better state."
—Scott Davis, retired Chairman and CEO, United Parcel Service, 2008–2014

"Ron Wallace writes about the values and leadership that helped establish a culture so that UPSers around the world understand that we are all part of something bigger than ourselves."
—Mike Eskew, retired Chairman and CEO, United Parcel Service, 2002–2007

"Terrific job by Ron Wallace in capturing the leadership characteristics and bedrock principles of UPS and the people of UPS. Many of us can relate to Ron's examples because we have been there ourselves."
—Jim Kelly, retired Chairman and CEO, United Parcel Service, 1997–2001

"Early in your career, in midcareer, or sitting on top, *read this book* if you want to be a more effective leader. It draws on the thoughts and principles of past UPS leaders as well as the experience of author Ron Wallace, whose strong business credentials cannot be denied."
—Kent C. "Oz" Nelson, retired Chairman and CEO, United Parcel Service, 1989–1996

"Ron Wallace has been there, done that, and now we have the book to prove it. *Leadership Lessons from a UPS Driver* has more practical wisdom than a Harvard MBA or an entire library of business texts. Wallace has produced a paint-by-numbers set for the aspiring executive. As a bonus, it is a practical bible on how to live a more fulfilling life."
—The Honorable Frank McKenna, former Canadian ambassador to the United States and former Premier of New Brunswick

"You can never read enough about inspirational life stories, just as you can never read enough about great leadership. This book has both!"
—Herman Cain, President and CEO, THE New Voice, Inc., and former Republican presidential candidate

"No matter what industry or field you work in, *Leadership Lessons from a UPS Driver* will change your approach to leadership in a most significant way. Ron's pragmatic and highly effective leadership skills will help you take your game to a completely new level. You'll achieve remarkable results if you use the easy-to-follow steps outlined in this book. I guarantee it."
—Kent G. Callahan, President and CEO, Investments & Retirement Division, Transamerica

"The powerful way Ron's personal experiences have been interwoven with inspiring and profound leadership truths is brilliant. I'm a better author and consultant from reading this book—I guarantee you will be a better leader! Saddle up and get ready for a great ride!"

—**Chip R. Bell, author of** *The 9½ Principles of Innovative Service*

"When someone has been a key leader for one of the world's most respected organizations, and it has over 400,000 employees, and he writes a book about the lessons he learned, it should be a must-read. UPS is the company, Ron Wallace is the man, and *Leadership Lessons from a UPS Driver* is the book. Thanks, Ron, for sharing your wisdom with the world!"

—**Mark Miller, Vice President, Leadership Development, Chick-fil-A, Inc., and coauthor of the international bestseller** *The Secret*

"Reading a book by a man who started at the bottom and worked his way up, as Ron did, interests me. A workhorse myself, I feel a strong kinship with him. He makes it clear that his book is for us workhorses. If you aspire to be effective, this book is for you. It is not for show horses. No matter your level of responsibility within your organization, his advice is applicable. If you are prepared to learn, you have found a good teacher."

—**Jimmy Collins, retired President and COO, Chick-fil-A, Inc., and author of** *Creative Followership*

"For decades, Ron Wallace displayed unique leadership abilities at UPS. This would ultimately lead him to being responsible for thousands of employees who had to get things done in complex situations every day. Whether you're a beginning or an experienced leader, Ron's book, *Leadership Lessons from a UPS Driver*, can change your life as well as the life of your organization. It's a leadership must-read."

—**Mark Levy, author of** *Accidental Genius*

"*Leadership Lessons from a UPS Driver* is a must-read for leaders at all levels as well as those who aspire to be leaders. The proven principles that worked for Ron Wallace in his exemplary career are detailed in a very practical manner. Ron's stories bring his leadership principles to life. Don't miss this opportunity to learn from an outstanding leader as you pursue a career of excellence."

—**John R. Patterson, innovative service consultant and speaker and coauthor of** *Wired and Dangerous*

"Finally, a book that hits the heart of doing what's right. A straightforward, no-holds-barred approach to leadership principles. A refreshing wake-up call for anyone leading others."

—**Emily Thomas Kendrick, President and CEO, Arrow Exterminators, Inc.**

Leadership Lessons
from a UPS Driver

LEADERSHIP LESSONS

LESSONS

— *from a* —

UPS DRIVER

DELIVERING A CULTURE OF WE, NOT ME

RON WALLACE

FORMER DELIVERY DRIVER AND PRESIDENT, UPS INTERNATIONAL

Berrett–Koehler Publishers, Inc.
a BK Business book

Berrett-Koehler Publishers, Inc.
1333 Broadway, Suite 1000
Oakland, CA 94612-1921
Tel: (510) 817-2277   Fax: (510) 817-2278   www.bkconnection.com

Ordering Information
Quantity sales. Special discounts are available on quantity purchases by corporations, associations, and others. For details, contact the "Special Sales Department" at the Berrett-Koehler address above.
Individual sales. Berrett-Koehler publications are available through most bookstores. They can also be ordered directly from Berrett-Koehler: Tel: (800) 929-2929; Fax: (802) 864-7626; www.bkconnection.com
Orders for college textbook/course adoption use. Please contact Berrett-Koehler: Tel: (800) 929-2929; Fax: (802) 864-7626.
Orders by U.S. trade bookstores and wholesalers. Please contact Ingram Publisher Services, Tel: (800) 509-4887; Fax: (800) 838-1149; E-mail: customer.service@ingram publisherservices.com; or visit www.ingrampublisherservices.com/Ordering for details about electronic ordering.

Berrett-Koehler and the BK logo are registered trademarks of Berrett-Koehler Publishers, Inc.

Printed in the United States of America

Berrett-Koehler books are printed on long-lasting acid-free paper. When it is available, we choose paper that has been manufactured by environmentally responsible processes. These may include using trees grown in sustainable forests, incorporating recycled paper, minimizing chlorine in bleaching, or recycling the energy produced at the paper mill.

Library of Congress Cataloging-in-Publication Data

Names: Wallace, Ron (Ronald G.), author.
Title: Leadership lessons from a UPS driver : delivering a culture of we,
    not me / Ron Wallace.
Description: Oakland, CA : Berrett-Koehler Publishers, Inc., [2016] |
    Includes bibliographical references and index.
Identifiers: LCCN 2015045482 | ISBN 9781626566880 (hardcover)
Subjects: LCSH: Wallace, Ron (Ronald G.) | United Parcel Service. | Chief
    executive officers—United States—Biography. | Express service—United
    States—Management. | Leadership.
Classification: LCC HE5903.U545 W35 2016 | DDC 658.4/092—dc23
LC record available at http://lccn.loc.gov/2015045482

First Edition
21 20 19 18 17 16   10 9 8 7 6 5 4 3 2 1

Cover/Jacket designer Radosław Krawczyk

Dedicated to UPS people around the world.

Words could never express what I feel for my many colleagues, mentors, and friends from UPS with whom I've had the privilege to serve over the years, and which ultimately led to the writing of this book.

Contents

Leadership Lessons
from a UPS Driver

Introduction

This book is about *delivering*. It's what UPS does every day of the week around the world.[1] Our friendly drivers in their sharp brown uniforms are the front line of our business. I can't tell you how many times I've heard people say that they love their UPS drivers and how much they look forward to receiving the packages the drivers deliver each day. The entire company—from the part-time employees to the chairman of the board—dedicates a tremendous amount of time and effort to support the endgame: the driver delivering the package.

Founded in 1907 and thriving more than ever, UPS is a very large family with a unique business culture. I am certain this distinctive culture is the reason for the company's remarkable success and is what keeps us in the number one spot for our industry even today.

I am proud to say that I was a UPS driver. Over the years, I worked my way up the ladder and eventually became president of UPS International, where I was responsible for UPS's operations in more than 220 countries and territories—directing thousands of managers at all levels. At different times, I served as chairperson or cochairperson of 33 boards of directors of highly successful companies across the globe. I was also one of a handful of people on the corporate management committee, responsible for the day-to-day operations of UPS and our more than 435,000 employees.

Leadership Matters

If I've learned anything during the long course of my life in business, it's this: leadership and a values-based culture matter. They are the key components that set great organizations apart from the pack. As the president of UPS International, I worked alongside many types of leaders from around the world, and I learned important lessons in leadership from each of them. The great ones, the less successful ones, and those who failed all taught me something. Whether they were in charge of small companies or international conglomerates, I witnessed firsthand what they did right and what they did wrong. I took to heart what those experiences taught me.

Reading a lot of theory is not why I buy books. I want facts, true stories, and sharp insights on leadership. To me, the most encouraging moments in life do not involve overly complicated, untested ideas. Rather, they are natural, timeless, and orderly progressions marked by accountability. Leadership is not rocket science. To build a high-performance team, use simple principles within a basic structure that everyone can easily understand.

To build a high-performance team, use simple principles within a basic structure that everyone can easily understand.

I have certainly made more than my share of mistakes through the years, and I'd like you to be the beneficiary of what I've learned from them. I hope that the lessons in this book will keep you from stepping on some of those same land mines and help propel you further and faster toward the attainment of your goals. If you've committed to venturing into the realm of leadership, you should know up front that your journey will take you down a winding road of small advances, painful setbacks, and even bigger victories.

The fact of the matter is that I learned the most important leadership lessons from people within my own company, UPS. As I discovered, a great recipe always means that certain ingredients simply cannot be substituted or left out.

What Brown Did for Me

One of the biggest things Brown did for me (UPS is affectionately known as "Brown," after the Pullman-brown paint color of the company's vehicles) was to give me a PhD in teamwork. The values-driven culture at UPS provided me with both a platform and a regimen for personal growth. It consistently stretched and strengthened my development as a leader. I knew that I'd arrived at UPS whenever I'd hear someone say, "You bleed Brown." Believe me, that's high praise.

It is the dedicated people who made the company successful, day in and day out, in the trenches, and often under some of the most adverse business and political conditions in the world. These hardworking men and women deserve the credit for the success we achieved.

UPS is a no-nonsense, no-frills company. Our objective today is the same as it was when the company was started: to provide the best possible service at the lowest possible rates. The UPS mentality is to be thrifty and keep an eye on the bottom line. We know it's the little things that make a big difference—like turning off the lights when we leave a room to reduce energy costs.

The UPS culture of treating one another as family has served us very well over the years. When leaders look at their team members in this light, the importance of using their influence to serve those with whom they work comes into sharp focus. Priorities turn into sincere concern for the well-being of others and foster the desire to motivate everyone to bring his or her very best to work each day, helping the organization to reach its full potential.

Unfortunately, many people promoted to leadership positions don't know where to begin, how to fight through the middle, or how to finish strong. Novices, and even some veterans, often lack an understanding of what it takes to be a leader. Perhaps you fall into this group and firmly believe you are capable of leading others, but you're not quite sure how to go about it. You begin to ask yourself questions like: *How do I influence others? Why do some leaders seem to soar, while others barely get off the ground? How do I get started and maintain an upward trajectory that will lead to professional and personal growth?*

This book has the answers. The leadership style described in *Leadership Lessons from a UPS Driver* is simple, it's direct, and it works. It's from the front line and reflects the values those of us in the UPS family hold dear. The straightforward and easy-to-understand lessons I present will enable you to get on your feet and then ride out the inevitable storms.

Just as the laws of physics describe the universe around us, there are core principles that give shape to the leadership world. If you adhere to them, they will lead you to the success you desire. And although the core values that guide you should remain true and unchanging—your North Star—there are always new things to be learned.

At the end of this book, you will find a study guide that you and your team can use to dive deeper into the key points presented in each chapter. Together, you will discover ways to get better at "delivering" what you do.

CHAPTER 1

Delivering a Culture

From $100 Startup to Global Company

I began my UPS career as a package delivery driver in northern Idaho and served in that position for six years before being promoted to supervisor. Each time I assumed a higher level of responsibility, my view of leadership changed. What never changed, however, was the imperative to *deliver*. That was always at the center of everything we did at UPS.

Before we examine the unique culture at UPS, let me tell you a little bit about the company itself. I don't believe it's possible to truly understand how a culture like this exists and thrives unless you know something about its origins. UPS began as the American Messenger Company on August 28, 1907 by two teenage boys named Jim Casey and Claude Ryan. They started with one bicycle and $100.00 they borrowed from a friend. Their six-by-seven-foot office was rented for $15.00 per month and was located in the basement of a saloon in Seattle, Washington. In 1919 the firm adopted its present name, United Parcel Service (UPS).

The group's initial vision was to build a small messenger service with just a few people delivering messages on foot, by streetcar, and by bicycle. Times were tough—so bad, in fact, that legend has it there were intense discussions about how to justify the purchase of a one-cent stamp.

Fast-forward to the present, and the stark difference in the business scale and sheer size of our far-flung operations is almost beyond comprehension. Today, UPS is a worldwide company serving more than 220 countries and territories with approximately 435,000 employees. It has more than 100,000 vehicles, 540 airplanes, and nearly 28,000 facilities. UPS delivers on average more than 18 million packages and envelopes a day, which translates into a rate of about 37,500 per minute or 625 per second. In addition to the package side of the operations, UPS has a growing supply-chain management solutions business that features services like logistics and distribution, transportation and freight (i.e., air, sea, ground, and rail), forwarding to and from 195 countries, international trade management, and customs brokerage. In the United States, UPS is the leading provider of less-than-truckload services coast-to-coast, using 5,800 vehicles and 20,000 trailers.

The UPS package car (*never* called a truck at UPS) and those heroes in brown uniforms (and socks) who deliver the packages each day are the first images that come to mind for most people when they think about our company. Although the uniforms worn by UPS drivers are similar around the world, the vehicles are not. For example, we use airboats in Vietnam, in some remote areas of Alaska packages reach their destination by dogsled. As you might imagine, gondolas are loaded with UPS packages in Venice; in Taiwan and Bangkok, tuk-tuks filled with UPS packages are a common sight throughout the crowded city streets.

A "Culture of We"

The UPS culture that we know today comes from a well-established, values-based environment formed in the company's early years. It was built on discipline, accountability, and the utmost respect for others at the outset. In 1929, our founder, Jim Casey, added to the company's policy book that UPS people would always be addressed by their first name. Jim was never too busy to talk to fellow employees at any level of the organization, and that practice quickly filtered down to the department managers and into their daily routines.

Greeting people, looking them in the eye, and listening to their concerns were things Jim loved to do, and he went out of his way to do them regularly. In Jim's view, the porter or car washer was just as important as the company's top-level executives. He had a genuine interest in people; whenever he met someone, he wanted to hear their stories and ideas for making the company better. He would never rush a conversation and would give the person his full and undivided attention. He openly described how he loved to learn from others and often incorporated their ideas into the business. *Servant leadership* is a popular term today. Serving others came naturally to Jim more than a hundred years ago, and he made it the cornerstone of our culture. He was all about "we" when it came to his UPS family.

My first encounter with Jim was in our UPS building in Seattle. It was late in the day, and I was the only person around. I was focused on hooking up a charger to a dead battery in one of our package cars when I suddenly felt someone standing next to me. I turned, and there he was, Jim Casey himself. I couldn't believe my eyes, and I'm sure he saw the look of shock on my face.

He stuck out his hand and said, "Hello, my name's Jim. What's yours?" Fortunately, I could remember it.

Then he said, "Here, let me help you. I'll hold the cables if you want to try to start it."

For a few seconds, I thought I was dreaming. Here was Jim Casey, our founder, a legend, and a man I idolized, getting his hands dirty while working alongside me at the very end of the day.

After the car started, Jim asked if I could take a few minutes to talk with him. He motioned toward a bench, where we sat and talked for about thirty minutes. During this conversation, he

> ### HOW LEADERSHIP LOOKS FROM HERE
> ## Leaders Walk the Talk
>
> Funny, isn't it, how the most memorable moment of my profes-
> sional life came down to a thirty-minute conversation on a bench
> in a maintenance shop. The vivid memory of the main man and
> little ol' me, just sitting around talking like members of one big,
> happy family, is forever burned in my brain. And, as it turned out,
> we *were* family.

asked me what I thought about "our" company and what ideas I might have to help us better serve our customers and become more efficient in our operations. Jim treated me as if I was *his* mentor, instead of the other way around. It was a day that I'll never forget and an experience that shaped my approach to leadership for the rest of my career.

Those who knew Jim best often observed that he was a walking contradiction. He was a dreamer, but he was also a doer. He was magnetic, but he avoided attention. He was confident, yet humble. He respected tradition, but change excited him. He was urgent and sometimes intense, but he always seemed calm and at peace. He was a visionary who could see the big picture but also a perfectionist who could zoom in on a misplaced comma.

The contradictions were vintage Jim Casey. However, he was, first and foremost, an avid learner and a devoted teacher. He wanted to better understand and be able to explain things for the sake of improvement.

Former UPS CEO George Smith said Jim taught him that the essence of leadership is just four basic things: to teach, to coach, to be taught, and to learn. Honestly, can it get any simpler than that?

Founding Principles That Have Endured

As unbelievable as it may seem, Jim Casey and his partners created policies, principles, and values in the early 1900s that continue to guide the company well over a hundred years later. As a constant reminder of this living heritage, the UPS policy book is referenced often today. In fact, it's still read at the start of staff meetings in UPS offices around the world. Our culture and founding principles are also frequently discussed in daily pre-work communication meetings with employees.

> To be truly effective, a company's culture has to dwell in the hearts and minds of the people charged with delivering its mission. They have to live and breathe their culture every day. It can't be reduced to some slogans plastered on a wall or a mission statement mounted in a nice picture frame. Rather, it must embody the soul of teamwork. It is up to the leaders to not only talk with their team members about those principles but also to live by them. To sustain a unique culture, all the components need to be present in the right proportions.

Creating an environment like this requires consistency and discipline. To succeed today and long into the future, you need to establish a culture based upon sound principles and policies that align with the values of your organization. At UPS, that strategic alignment is demonstrated in the following bedrock principles.

Establish a culture based upon sound principles and policies that align with the values of your organization.

People: Treat Everyone Equally

At UPS, we take a sincere interest in the well-being of our team members and treat everyone equally. In the words of Jim Casey:

The policy of impartiality means that everybody is treated equally; everybody has an equal opportunity; one person is on a par with all others; one can advance only because of more capability than others.[2]

A major factor in providing everyone with an equal opportunity to grow and rise in the ranks is the practice of not hiring relatives or friends, avoiding the potential for favoritism. In addition, our culture is built upon the belief that our people come first. For example, there is an open-door policy that gives all workers access to their managers.

UPS does not believe in titles per se and, as I mentioned, encourages everyone to be on a first-name basis. That is the expectation for our managers, although there are some other exceptions due to cultural considerations in countries outside the United States. We try to be as informal as possible whenever it's appropriate. Accordingly, as I alluded to earlier, it is not unusual for a car washer to call the CEO by their first name and vice versa. It's the family culture upbringing. Although UPSers have different responsibilities, we are still all in it together, working toward the same goals.

Once the people you deal with recognize what you do springs from an honest heart, they will be surprisingly strong in their support of you.

- They will believe what you say.
- They will do what you want.
- They will give you their loyalty.
- They will trust and follow you.[3]

Pride: Show Pride in the Company and Pride in the Work

Someone once asked me to pick one word that best describes why UPS is so special. The answer was easy. I had lived it every day as an employee, and I still live it today. That word is *pride*. We show pride in the company and pride in the work that we do.

Of course, pride can be instilled in many different ways. At UPS, it comes from professionalism, quality service, and the quest for perfection in everything we do. For instance, our appearance standards help us present an image that UPSers are proud of and yield something tangible and continuous that the public depends on. It's hard to quantify exactly why something so simple is so inspiring in its own understated way, but the results confirm that professional appearance matters.

> We show pride in the company and pride in the work that we do.

Our customers often say that they know they can trust UPS because of our reputation. A big part of that comes from the pride within our ranks and the way we consistently perform so well in all the small things.

Appearance: Make a Positive Visual Impression

Quality is largely a matter of appearance. People judge us by the visual and mental impression they get. If those impressions are to be favorable, we must have the appearance of doing a good job.[4]

From the beginning, UPS decided it would be a company that would send customers a strong message of assurance and quality by making a positive visual impression on the public. This belief, and the resulting emphasis on making positive impressions, extends not only to uniforms for drivers but also to sparkling-clean package cars, offices, and buildings. Just as they did more than one hundred years ago, today's drivers must meet these strict appearance standards, including good personal hygiene, cleaned and pressed uniforms, and shined shoes.

When a store executive sees one of our cars with dented fenders, or a scratched body, or a car in need of paint, what kind of impression does that create? And whose fault is it? The driver's? No. It's the fault of someone higher up for failing to have an inspection system that will detect such defects immediately and have them corrected before the car goes out on the road.[5]

✳   Simply said, it is the leaders' job to "see it—own it—solve it—do it" when they encounter a problem or an opportunity to improve something.

Communication: Build a "Culture of We"

UPS employees gather for a daily meeting (known as a pre-work communication meeting, or PCM) with their supervisor prior to starting work, where they hear current company news and other topics of interest that may relate to their particular group.

During the PCM in the operating centers, managers have an opportunity to inspect their drivers to ensure they meet the company's appearance standards. Although these meetings usually last about three minutes, they keep employees informed about significant company news.

Keep employees informed about significant company news.

Open communication helps to avoid unpleasant surprises and workplace rumors. Keeping employees informed and engaged in these quick pre-work meetings is an excellent way to start the day.

Owned by the Managers, Managed by the Owners

UPS's managers (and many of the company's employees) own UPS stock. This ownership structure has produced a tremendously positive effect on the day-to-day operations as well as on the company's long-term goals of growth and financial stability.

Promotion from Within

UPS believes that managers who start with the organization and rise through its ranks are likely to be more committed, aligned, and knowledgeable than those brought in laterally from the outside. We promote from within to ensure that the company can pass on our legacy and culture seamlessly from one generation to the next.

When we invest in people, we're looking at it as a lifetime decision. This is why the hiring process is so important and should never be rushed. We look for people who want a career with us, not just a job for a limited time. This is a huge part of the success formula at UPS.

The part-time loader in a hub could well be the future CEO, and UPS's strategy is to hold on to people who show potential throughout their careers. Most new hires start as part-time employees and work their way up through the ranks.

Following our tradition, the management team at UPS, including the CEO and management committee, started as drivers, part-time loaders, car washers, and clerks. As part of the promotion process, all must spend time as package car drivers or as driver helpers to understand the heart of our business. With an active succession plan, we always know where we'll draw the next level of leadership from within the company.

Constructive Dissatisfaction

No matter how successful a company is, its employees should never be satisfied. Once we do something well, we should start over and figure out how to do it better. Good companies adapt to changing conditions; great ones stay ahead of them. They don't deny that perplexing conditions exist, nor do they pretend that markets will never be uncertain or unkind. In fact, they embrace those realities and the potential for a storm by staying nimble and agile. They are "constructively dissatisfied." Leaders make conditions; they don't become victims of them.

It is always the little things in business that matter most, and one of those "little" things that Jim Casey noticed and remarked on remains true for most organizations today. It went like this:

> I think we should test and check many of our present practices. Some of the things can be eliminated, and some can be improved. Among other things, I think we are using many useless reports. I think we are filling out forms that don't need to be filled out. I think we are doing a lot of work that accomplishes nothing, and we ought to study that and dispense with it as quickly as we can.[6]

Managers should not be *reporters* of problems; they need to be *fixers* of problems and take corrective action on the spot. If they need help, they should sound the alarm. No one should turn his or her back on anything that is not up to strict company standards.

Although UPS isn't perfect, it may be worth noting that 88 percent of the companies on the Fortune 500 list in 1955 are now dead and buried. So how can a company that traces its roots back to 1907 still be going strong today? How has UPS managed to place at the top of almost every list for best places to work, strong management, and quality of investment, year after year?

The answer is a combination of factors, but recognizing our shortcomings and being "constructively dissatisfied" would have to be towards the top of that list.

How *You* Can Deliver

- Develop an atmosphere of mutual respect and trust. When appropriate, call people by their first names.
- Do more than talk company culture; live it and make it come alive within your team.
- Make sure that your employees hear company news and anything that directly affects them from you first.
- Remember that high standards of appearance represent you and your company. Be strict; do not compromise.
- When possible, provide a platform that allows everyone to be owners, not just employees.

CHAPTER 2

Building a Successful Team

Play Your "Best Five," Not Your Five Best

Great teams don't just show up fully prepared and ready to accomplish the mission. The best team builders create a seamless alignment among the team members that becomes the glue keeping all of them working together.

The most successful team builders are masters at establishing trust and respect among teammates. At the end of the day, they are the first to acknowledge and celebrate the combined efforts that brought success to the entire group. They are also the first ones to take the blame when things don't go well.

Make no mistake about it: ability matters, and you should do everything you can to attract, develop, and retain great talent. But if you have to choose between talent and chemistry, choose chemistry. In most cases where it takes a group of people to get the job done correctly, I believe chemistry is as important as education, experience, or skills.

In sports, as in business, teamwork trumps talent nine times out of ten. Legendary UCLA basketball coach John Wooden used to say, "I don't play my five best, I play my best five." The "best five" is shorthand for the ones who work best together and achieve synergy and chemistry.

When people combine their efforts and create results that are greater than the sum of their individual contributions, something magical occurs. The entire team benefits and so does the organization. Those people who are committed to the end goal are far more concerned about the team winning than they are about embellishing their individual statistics.

Every person in a leadership role faces the same challenge: which "five" to assign to their organization's most important projects. Effective leaders know

To accomplish your goals, identify your "best five" and play them.

that playing your five best (i.e., most talented) employees can be a mistake if they don't work well together. To accomplish your goals, identify your "best five" and play them.

Promote Teamwork, Not Superstars

In the summer of 2015, the largest U.S. television audience ever for any soccer game—30.9 million at its peak—watched as the U.S. women's team celebrated a well-deserved victory in the seventh FIFA Women's World Cup.[7]

After the team lifted the gold trophy in what might very well be the greatest win in the history of women's soccer, the media swarmed the coaching staff and players with questions that consistently sought the same insights: "What makes your team so good?" "What is the reason for your success?"

As the rapid-fire questions poured in, the responses from coaches and players began to repeat a similar theme and tone as well. "We are a team—no heroes, no superstars." "We depend on each other, and we win as a team." "We never give up; we believe in each other."

Indeed, it is the same story and the same lessons, learned repeatedly, regardless of the sport or the country. Even in the world of individual sports competition, the winners, from boxers to golfers to race car drivers, are quick to give credit to their coaches, trainers, managers, and the team of people tirelessly working behind the scenes to help them be successful.

Mentor Your Team for Success

When positive things happen, those moments require a readiness that is more than just effort and determination. There is also an unmistakable element of being ready for whatever life lobs at you. To prepare yourself for additional responsibility, you need a mentor. Whom do you know who can help you learn the ropes? Can you enlist the support of someone who has walked in your shoes and has experience in the same or a similar job?

For example, a new medical intern would be wise to ask for help from a veteran nurse who has worked in a hospital for years. If the intern is fortunate, that nurse may become his or her mentor and likely will teach things that go well beyond what's in books or taught in school. And being street smart is just as important as being book smart. Those people who served for decades on the front lines know best what upper-level managers may have long forgotten.

Because there are many types of business, from startups with only a few employees to multibillion-dollar companies employing thousands of people around the globe, one leadership style does not fit all circumstances. Would the same approach work for a small group of accountants as it would for a professional football team? No, probably not.

In reality, though, the principles these organizations employ may not be all that different. They each are charged with leading human beings—people who have real lives away from the job, personal and professional ambitions, unique talents, and insecurities—toward a stated purpose and vision.

Do Whatever Is Necessary in Extraordinary Circumstances

Organizations are successful because people work together as a team: no heroes, no superstars. They trust and depend upon each other to do the right thing because teammates don't let one another down when it counts the most. The discipline and the will to push through challenges begin with the proper mindset. If you believe you can do it and put your heart and soul into it, you can reach any goal and overcome almost any obstacle.

North to Alaska

Although UPS has been around since 1907, we did not deliver to all states until 1975. I was a division manager in Seattle when Jack Casey (no relation to Jim Casey), the district manager, called me into his office one day and asked me to head up a team that would open the state of Alaska for UPS. He said to take plenty of warm clothes and to be prepared to stay there for at least a year. *A year in freezing Alaska, thousands of miles from home?* That certainly made my day.

Setting Up the New Operation

I quickly put together a diverse team with members who each had a different skill set and, with the help of several staff departments, began making plans for the opening. We prepared the normal operating plans necessary to open a new business, including a detailed market analysis showing volume estimates. All the expected necessities, people, delivery vehicles, and facilities were based on the planned volume; leaving nothing to chance, we forecasted around 50 packages per day for the first month, with a gradual but steady increase thereafter.

A few weeks later, our team arrived in Anchorage and began to set up the new operation. We rented a small portion of a building at the airport, hired employees, leased a few small vans, and signed up as many new customers as we could.

Opening Day! Great! . . . Uh Oh

Opening day came upon us fast, and we were confident that we were ready to launch our new business in the great state of Alaska. After the ribbon-cutting ceremony with employees, local VIPs, and the media present, we proudly watched the first UPS aircraft land and taxi to just a few hundred feet from our building. The cargo doors opened, and the crew unloaded one air container from the plane onto a dolly, followed by another, and then another, and then another. I began to lose count and started to feel sick to my stomach.

My mind flashed back to that market study that indicated we would get around 50 packages per day for the first month. We were staring at far more than 1,500 packages on the first day alone, a full year ahead of the original estimate.

We Urgently Needed Our "Best Five" Team

In an instant, we realized just how bad our projections were. I say *our*, but I was the one in charge and I really blew it. We were caught off guard and unprepared and had to make some things happen fast. Our small team of drivers and trainers did the best they could and worked late into the night.

Knowing that the initial flood of packages would only increase in number as the days went on, and realizing we had vastly underestimated the need for our services in the area, I called Jack and pleaded for help. After a few minutes of silence, followed by a few groans, he said he would call me back.

An hour later, he called and said the cavalry was on its way. Six large UPS package cars were being loaded with bedding and supplies, including food and water, extra tires, and plenty of tools and spare parts. He told me there would be two drivers per vehicle and they would drive straight through from Seattle to Anchorage, stopping only for fuel. One driver would sleep while the other one drove.

A few days later, at 3:00 a.m., there was a knock on my door. When I opened it, there stood a dozen tired and ragged UPSers who had just driven more than 2,000 miles almost nonstop, including 1,400 miles on the rugged dirt and gravel road called the ALCAN Highway. After sending them off for some badly needed showers and sleep, I got dressed as fast as I could and headed to the parking lot, anxious to check out the newly arrived package cars.

As I neared the parking lot, I could not believe what I saw. Those six package cars were mostly gray primer with just a little bit of brown paint here and there at the roofline. They were badly dented, and most of them had shattered windshields. The brutal beating they had endured during their long, grueling trip was obvious. I was tempted to call Jack and tell him "thanks a lot"; but at that moment, I wasn't sure how secure my job was, so I left well enough alone.

A few hours later, we dragged our weary new arrivals out of bed and welcomed them to America's last frontier by putting them to work. After a quick briefing, I sent a few of them to take the beat-up cars to local body shops, with instructions to pay whatever was necessary to make the cars roadworthy and looking like new. Of course, we needed the work done yesterday. I assigned the HR manager and one of the local supervisors the task of hiring additional, permanent drivers from the local area as fast as they could.

We sent the others to rent as many vans as they could and meet back at the UPS building, where they became our delivery drivers and trainers for the immediate future. It was a fire drill for sure, but I knew we could pull it off because that is what Brown-blooded people do.

Within a few weeks, we were back on our feet with a fully trained workforce driving newly painted UPS package cars. Although we really missed the mark on the initial volume projections, we learned some valuable lessons. In the end, our dedicated Alaska team, with the help of our partners from Seattle, proved that determined people working together can accomplish anything. We hadn't fielded our "best five"; we had fielded our "best fifteen."

We Did What Was Necessary in Extraordinary Circumstances

We had begun laying the foundation for our success in Alaska years before our first shipment arrived there. Our commitment to the UPS values I've already discussed is the reason we overcame the challenges we faced.

We opened Alaska, not with great projections, but with great attitude and drive in the face of staggering obstacles. We believed we could do it; we put our heart and soul into it; and we proved that we could reach any goal, overcome almost any obstacle—even the ALCAN Highway. If we hadn't believed that we could do it, then we would have been destined to fail, our path a self-fulfilling prophecy.

HOW LEADERSHIP LOOKS FROM HERE

Leaders Lead Lives

As a driver, my thinking typically focused on the task and on the day-to-day list of what I had to accomplish to do a good job. As I moved up in the ranks, my thinking had to adjust as my scope of responsibility widened. I not only had to do a good job myself, but I now had to ensure that the other team members assigned to me performed well too.

Being a leader is a position of great trust; you have proven you are worthy of being given a chance to serve others in a powerful role. But leading is a sacred responsibility for the lives of the people who are under your supervision. I sought to make the most of the opportunity. I adjusted my view of leadership, making sure it took in the people whose lives were now my responsibility.

Jack Casey had served as a great mentor for me. When crises hit, he did not panic nor did he look up "what to do when package volume exceeds projections" in the training manuals. With no time to spare, he just did what had to be done and made things happen. That is what leaders do. They have the courage to do whatever is necessary in extraordinary situations, a lesson I would have ample opportunity to apply throughout my career.

Have the courage to do whatever is necessary in extraordinary situations.

Be a Leader, Not a Boss

One of the greatest lessons I learned at UPS is that a boss is not a leader. Sure, you might have the title or rank, and you may even believe you have earned the right to order others around to get things done. But don't be fooled for one minute. Making people bosses does not magically transform them into leaders. Most failed leaders did not know the difference between bossing and leading.

Know the difference between bossing and leading.

Leaders take charge and inspire others to do the right thing regardless of circumstances. While maintaining high energy and focus, they lead by quiet example and unassuming acts of service, reaching beyond themselves to ensure their teams have their full support. They make sure that all members have exactly what they need to do the job correctly. They do everything possible to make the job interesting and fun. They keep their people engaged and challenged. Along with improving their teams, they work on continued self-improvement: self-study, mentorship, learning from their own and others' mistakes. They have a clear vision and are calculated risk takers who accept responsibility and are willing to be judged by their successes or failures in reaching specific objectives.

The Characteristics of Effective Leaders
Effective leader behaviors include:
- Strong character, integrity, high energy, competence.
- A servant leader mentality.
- A balanced approach led by fairness in all interpersonal dealings.

- Willingness to take risks and be accountable for their actions.
- Ability to work well with people, welcoming and encouraging input.
- Modesty and desire to give credit to others.
- Initiative and acceptance of change.
- Vision and focus.

Leaders can be trusted to live and succeed—as well as perish or fail—without losing their integrity along the way. They understand the importance of building and maintaining positive relationships with their team members. They know they can create value in the world by creating value in others.

Bosses, on the other hand, take shortcuts and are consistently self-centered in their approach, with little regard for the needs of others. They wield their power to coerce and intimidate in order to get things done. They do not get the most out of their people because people who fear for their jobs cannot be simultaneously energetic and solution-minded partners.

Bosses are not team builders, and they seldom enjoy genuine and lasting loyalty from their followers. Their careers are normally short-lived, and the damage left in their wake often causes organizational distrust. They typically blame others for their own shortcomings, take the credit for successes generated by their team's hard work, and create an atmosphere devoid of what all great teams need for fuel: unselfishness.

Bosses and ineffective managers often have one or more of the following characteristics:

- An unhealthy and overwhelming desire to be popular and in control.

- Willingness to sacrifice their integrity to accomplish their goals.
- Inability to work well with others.
- Hesitation about listening to and accepting the views of others.
- Avoidance of risk and responsibility (flying under the radar).
- Consideration of their own interests first, team members second.
- Lack of initiative and inability to accept change easily.
- Limited vision and focus.

Imagine if we had to open Alaska under a boss. Our efforts could have failed if either Jack Casey or I had acted like a boss, or if we had "bossed" the team members we were asking to give so much. Our team could not have pulled off the extraordinary feats without a shared, deeply held vision and the whole team's faith in its other members and leaders.

It's okay to enjoy your accomplishments, but don't ever think that your achievements make you better than those around you. Nor should you ever think that it was you alone who got you there.

It's obvious many things go into producing the kind of leader people are willing and eager to follow. Maybe the key is realizing there is more power in *we* than in *me*. Maybe the cornerstone is being a better listener than a talker. Maybe the one essential ingredient is being willing to get out on the front line with your people. Maybe it's as simple as being a person of integrity.

> *Don't ever think that your achievements make you better than those around you. Nor should you ever think that it was you alone who got you there.*

Whatever it is, as a leader *you* set the pace, and your people will follow whatever example you set—good or bad.

If you hope to accomplish something great, you are going to need some help. You will need to become an expert at building a team so strong that its members can get the job done even when you're not around. Good leaders believe in themselves; great leaders believe in the potential of others and convince *them* to believe in themselves.

You are ultimately responsible for creating the foundation and framework for your organization's success. That means selecting, training, and nurturing all members of your team so they will not only exceed your expectations but their own as well.

In the next chapter, you'll discover why I knew when I landed in the UPS culture that I was very blessed.

How *You* Can Deliver

- Play your "best five," not your five best. Promote teamwork to accomplish the shared goal. Don't settle for a splintered group of superstars.
- Bring heart and passion to the game.
- Ensure that all members of your team are aligned with one another—and with the objectives.
- Manage your team so that all members trust one another and are held accountable, both individually and as a group.
- Take charge and do what is right.
- Seek out a mentor at every stage in your career. Their support can be invaluable.
- Give others credit for successes and create a culture of *we*, not *me*.

CHAPTER 3

Divine Intervention

D oing the right thing is something I learned at a very young age growing up in the small town of Lewiston, Idaho. Life was good back then, but for my mother and me, it wasn't always easy. When I was six years old, my father left us; and, at times, it was difficult to get by on mother's meager wages. It was no fun at the time, but as I look back, I can appreciate the things I learned from those early days of my childhood.

Because of the need to help make ends meet, when I was about ten years old, I started working odd jobs on weekends and during the summers.

A few years later, I landed a job working as a ranch hand for the summer. I worked alongside cowboys from the crack of dawn until well after the sun had set. Part of that job gave me the opportunity to be involved in several cattle drives. Yep, that meant horses, chaps, boots, spurs—the whole bit. The long days I spent out on the range caused me to grow up fast and helped me to understand not only the value of a dollar but also of a strong work ethic and the importance of teamwork.

After leaving my summer job on the ranch, I returned to school and found a part-time job working nights at a local service station. I was paid 50 cents an hour but enjoyed all sorts of financial incentives, such as earning a dime for an oil change or for fixing a flat tire.

While most of my friends were off doing the fun things teenagers typically do after school, I continued to work a variety of jobs. I was always looking for ways to make more money, and I readily jumped from one job to the next.

Then high school graduation arrived, and with few jobs available in my hometown, I wandered off to find decent full-time employment. I soon found myself living with my father hundreds of miles away in Washington. I couldn't believe I got the first job I applied for, as it was full time and paid very well. I thought it was because of my résumé; I later found out no one else in town wanted it because it involved driving a tanker truck loaded with highly toxic chemicals. To add to my newfound wealth, at night I worked in my father's restaurant. Not content with my income from just two jobs, on weekends I had a third job installing insulation in new homes. I guess the locals didn't want that job either. These were the blisters-on-my-hands, working-from-sunup-to-sundown kind of jobs. I learned to be resourceful and to do the work that others thought was below their status.

This approach served me well for a while, but I didn't see much future for myself with these employers, so I packed up and headed back to Idaho. Instead of moving back in with my mother, I decided it was time to be on my own, so a friend and I took up residency in the storeroom of a local dive bar. Sleeping bags were our beds, candles provided our light, and the hose for cleaning mops was our shower. In return for such fine accommodations—including rats for pets, and barroom brawls for a nightly soundtrack—we had the privilege of cleaning up the messy bar after closing time. That was fine with us—we were young, single, and not all that bright; but we were grateful we didn't have to pay any rent.

Eventually, the excitement of the independent life began to lose its luster, so I moved back in with my mother. As it turned out, that was one of the best things I ever did. I was not that great at being on my own at the time, but that didn't keep me from working every possible minute. I worked the night shift—first in a food-processing plant and then in a sawmill—and I always worked double shifts on the weekends, as they paid time and a half for the second eight hours.

But it didn't last.

My job was eliminated, and me along with it. Soon afterward, I was dead broke. As if that wasn't enough, I was engaged to be married.

Marry Me—I'm Unemployed

With no job, no money, and no plan, I had no idea what I was going to do. I had fallen to a new low.

Then a miracle occurred, and I am convinced to this day it was divine intervention. Whatever the source was, UPS came to my rescue.

On the night before my wedding, the phone rang. It was a gentleman from UPS asking me if I was still interested in working for them. I had forgotten about having applied for a job with this company a few months earlier.

Though I had no idea what UPS was or even what they did, I couldn't say "Yes!" fast enough. I didn't care how much they paid, what my job would be, or the hours I would work. I was desperate. I needed work, *any* work, and I needed it fast.

The man on the phone told me to report to work first thing Monday morning. It was perfect timing. I was getting married on Saturday and starting a new job on Monday morning. My prayers were answered. The honeymoon would have to wait. We had rent to pay.

Ron, Meet UPS

When I arrived at UPS early Monday morning, I was promptly greeted by a neatly groomed man in a well-pressed suit and tie. He had an infectiously positive attitude and seemed genuinely excited to meet me.

He shook my hand and said, "Just call me Fred." For the next thirty minutes, Fred asked me about my family, my hobbies, my favorite sports, and all of the things he thought might be important to me.

What were my first impressions of Fred? He treated me more like a friend and less like a new employee on his first day on the job. He related to me on a real and personal level, the furthest thing from being a "boss." I'd never worked for anyone like him before.

Later on, while describing his role at UPS, Fred told me: "Although I am your trainer, we are more like partners and we will learn together. I know the package business, and you know the town and the people. I am going to teach you all the proper methods that will make you a successful package car driver. No pressure—in fact we are going to have fun—and when I feel you are ready to go out on your own, I will get out of your way."

Soon the other new employees arrived. Fred gathered us and told us inspiring stories about the company's founder, Jim Casey, and the early days of the company as well as the vision of the firm. He explained that UPS considers the people working for them to be family, *not* hired hands.

I had an immediate sense of belonging. I knew this was going to be more than just another job to hold me over until a better one came along. This was a *people* company with a rich heritage. Fred made it clear that we must work together as a team and learn to trust and depend on one another.

After explaining the high expectations he had for each of us, Fred showed us the UPS package car. I'll never forget seeing that shiny brown package car for the first time. I was so impressed that I could only stand there and admire it, wondering if I might get a chance to drive it someday.

From there, things only got better as the day went on. I was issued my brown uniform with the same UPS shield I had just seen moments earlier on the side of that car. I felt a huge sense of pride well up inside of me to know I was going to be part of a great company.

Fred explained that UPS was committed to making a difference in the lives of their employees. I knew then and there that this company was special, but what I didn't know was that my life was about to be changed forever.

Early Leadership Lessons

Several years later, as I started to rise in the organization, I learned that Fred was not an aberration: he was very much like the other UPS leaders I met along the way. He was modest, professional, showed strong character, and was passionate about his job. Fred was very insistent on "doing things by the book," which in UPS language means doing it the one and only best way. This is how UPS operates, and it translates into maximum efficiency.

Determined People Look for Solutions

In principle, the UPS environment is very structured and disciplined. Every aspect of each job has one specific, best way it's done, and each part of the method demands precision. At the same time, people are encouraged to search for better ways to do things. I discovered that in most cases, UPS people typically find common sense solutions to complex problems.

As you've probably guessed by now, UPS founder Jim Casey was the consummate leader. When it came to business, hard work

---

Leaders Base Relationships on Trust and Mutual Respect

After barely three months with the company, I was appointed lead driver and placed in charge of our little enterprise. Our small group of eight was on its own, with the closest manager several hundred miles away. Suddenly I had more to manage than just me.

As my time there passed and my opportunities increased, I began to learn everything I could about UPS and the company's leadership philosophy. With no experience in supervising others, I soon realized that no matter where you work, whether it's in a small town in Idaho or the corporate headquarters in Atlanta, leadership isn't really all that complicated. In fact, most of it is common sense.

To the extent that I've been successful as a leader, it is directly attributed to those early lessons and the fact that I learned the UPS way of doing things right from the start. UPS taught me both how to lead and how to follow. But the most important lessons I learned were about human behavior and how to inspire and encourage others to give their best possible effort. To this day, I believe that the single most important thing that every leader does is to establish relationships based on trust and mutual respect.

Establish relationships based on trust and mutual respect.

---

and long hours were part of his daily routine. He did not want to hear that problems could not be fixed, and his managers learned to look for solutions instead of excuses.

Jim firmly believed and told others, "Determined people make conditions—they do not allow themselves to become victims of them."[8] He wanted the leadership team to make decisions and be responsible for their actions. In other words, he wanted them to step out and lead. He trusted people to do the right thing, the right way.

Leaders Have Integrity

Leaders have integrity and do the right thing. This is the essence of leadership. Whether it's called honesty, ethics, character, or doing what's right, integrity consistently ranks at the top of the list of what people look for in a leader. In a study conducted by *U.S. News & World Report* and Harvard University's Center for Public Leadership, 95 percent of respondents said that integrity is either an

Have integrity and do the right thing. This is the essence of leadership.

extremely important or a very important characteristic of a good leader.

Character Comes First

There are numerous pieces to the leadership puzzle, but great leaders recognize that character will always be their most valuable asset.

Regardless of what anyone else does, great leaders stay true to fostering an environment where character is king. One of the biggest ironies in business is how so many people fail to see that when you put character first, the rest will follow.

Contemporary wisdom seems to suggest that character must be sacrificed sometimes and corners cut to enhance the bottom line. This ends-justifies-the-means mentality is a slow-motion culture killer.

Part of having good character as a leader is honoring your team members when they achieve successful outcomes. The best leaders understand that more gets done when you don't care who gets the credit.

By nature, UPSers go out of their way to recognize the accomplishments of others and shy away from taking any credit for themselves. Modesty at UPS is an understatement, and the "we, not me" mantra is a fundamental piece of the culture.

Successes Are "Ours," Not "Mine"

In the course of being led effectively, and while leading the members of my team, I found that the best leaders make a real difference in the lives of their people because they genuinely care about them.

Effective leaders understand that every single person makes the company what it is. True leaders refer to their organizations' successes as "ours," not "mine." They have a unique ability to show team members that they *are* the company and not merely employees of it.

Show team members that they are the company and not merely employees of it.

As I mentioned, the best leaders don't draw attention to themselves but instead focus on getting things done through others. To complement their own unique experience and talents, they make a point of recruiting passionate people who bring diverse knowledge and skills to the table. They build teams that achieve exceptional synergy and results by capitalizing on each member's strengths, giving them the authority they need to make decisions and then trusting them to carry out the organization's mission.

Your Success Is Bigger Than You

At UPS, as in any successful organization, results trump behavior and effort. By surrounding yourself with others who have the skills and talents you lack, you form a partnership of excellence with each member of your team.

One note of caution, however. To succeed, you need people who will take command, take action, and then be willing to operate in the *take-calculated-risks zone*. They are your "A" team and need little to no supervision. You'll see several UPS people operating in the *take-calculated-risks zone* as this book unfolds.

These people make things happen. Surrounding yourself with people like them is one of the most important keys to long-term success no matter where you work.

Your success is bigger than you are. Ultimately, your team will make or break you. Your team makes a difference, and building a strong team matters more than almost anything else you will do.

How *You* Can Deliver

- Be welcoming and supportive to new employees—your first impression on them will last forever.
- Be a person of integrity, the number-one trait employees want in their leaders.
- Look for solutions, not excuses.
- Remember that determined people make conditions; they do not become victims of them.
- Build a strong team, which will matter more than almost anything else you do. Your team will make or break you.

Build a strong team, which will matter more than almost anything else you do.

CHAPTER 4

Developing Your Team's Unique Talents

Find Your *It*

To manage yourself, you first have to understand what unique talents you bring to your business, your community, and the world. This means figuring out your *It*, the thing you were born to do.

Don't be someone you're not.

One key lesson I've learned is that when you try to do things outside of your skill set, you'll end up frustrating not only yourself but your coworkers as well. No matter how tempting it may be to imitate the style of another leader, don't be someone you're not.

Coming to grips with this truth, though, demands that you first answer some tough questions about yourself before moving on in your career.

> What is the one thing you have the greatest potential to master? Where within you is the greatness waiting to happen? What wakes you up early and keeps you up late? What stirs your passion?
>
> Honest answers to these questions will lead you to your "*It*." If you hope to move from good to great in your life, you must zero in on this one thing. Even if this means switching careers to do something that truly gets you excited to go to work each day, do it. You will be amazed at how your life changes for the better.

A deeper self-inventory requires that you ask yourself these questions:

- *Is It fulfilling?* If your *It* results in a sense of satisfaction and accomplishment, you will stay motivated even during the tough times.
- *Is It fruitful?* If what drives you makes a positive difference in the lives of others, you have discovered why you are here.
- *Is It fun?* You will be great only at something you enjoy doing.
- *Is It bringing you affirmation?* If others notice or benefit from it, it is your strength and a positive reinforcement of your leadership.

Help Team Members Identify What Drives Them

When you help people find and fulfill their "*It*," that one thing that drives them, you build up an energy and level of commitment that will give a tremendous boost to the power of the team. Focus on fostering an environment where each individual can readily see how their own talents fit within the context of the entire team's objectives. Encourage, even challenge, your team to identify what they are passionate about; then get out of their way and let them do it.

During my six-year stint with UPS in Germany, I had a division manager in my district named Danny. He was usually the first person at work in the morning and the last to leave at night, but he was far from an office dweller. He was street-smart and knew how to get amazing results by inspiring his people.

Danny was an expert team builder and could always be found with his sleeves rolled up, working side by side with his team. He made a point of regularly connecting with his 50 managers and the more than 1,500 employees under his supervision.

Danny had his hands in everything, and every part of his operation from top to bottom had to meet his high expectations. His enthusiasm was contagious, as were his work ethic and principles, and he never wavered on them. He knew what it took to get the job done and get it done right.

Because of Danny's passion for the business and his people, he had fun at work. People who have fun on the job tend to be very productive. He set the tone and led the charge, and his people followed him as if he were the Pied Piper.

Danny's operation consistently had the best results in the country by a wide margin: best service, lowest cost, lowest turnover, best safety record, and a long list of everything else that we measured. You could sense great pride and high morale in every facet of Danny's operation.

> *People who have fun on the job tend to be very productive.*

When my other managers asked me how they could improve, I would just say, "Do what Danny does. Go watch and copy him." And what did Danny do? He did the same things most effective leaders do. He motivated others. He supported his people. He had high standards, and he held people accountable for meeting them. In simpler terms, he outworked everyone else.

We often hear "Work smarter, not harder." This is clever advice, and the right thing to do if you can, but clever words are not always completely true. It takes hard work and many long hours to accomplish your goals, no matter how smart you are working. When I think of Danny, I know that the right answer is to "Work smarter *and* harder."

I remember one manager telling me about the night the car washer did not show up for work. Danny happened to be in the

> ### HOW LEADERSHIP LOOKS FROM HERE
> ## Leaders Spread Their Enthusiasm
>
> Attitude is the one area where you have total control. When you show up every day with your best self fully engaged, you are bound to spread enthusiasm and a can-do attitude to the rest of your team.
>
> Enthusiasm is wind in a sail—it keeps the ship moving forward. People need to see that you are both committed to and excited about the work your team does. They will take their cues from you. When you believe in your people, they will believe in you.

building. Without hesitating, he changed his clothes and spent the night washing cars. That was Danny. He did whatever it took. Titles and position meant very little to him.

However, working harder makes a difference only when, like Danny, you are passionate about what you do. If you are, you will exude enthusiasm for your work, and your employees will take notice and follow suit.

Danny obviously had mastered self-management. He could manage others artfully because he knew his own values and the UPS principles and had internalized them all to become a cheerful, inspiring manager to his people.

It All Begins with Self-Leadership

Without question, the most difficult person I ever had to lead during my many years at UPS was someone I knew very well—*me*. Some hard lessons early in my career showed me that I clearly had a lot to learn. You have to know how to manage yourself before you begin managing others.

You have to know how to manage yourself before you begin managing others.

I vividly recall one particular afternoon about six months after I'd transitioned to the role of operations supervisor. The center clerk came into my office and announced she was resigning. It took me completely by surprise.

I asked her, "Why are you doing this?"

Her answer was something I never forgot: "Because you're working almost around the clock—killing yourself over delivering a box—and I don't want to be buried with you!"

I was stunned.

After I collected my thoughts, I asked the clerk to explain. She said I'd been driving myself and everyone else around me to the breaking point because I had gotten far too demanding and much too short in my responses to my team. I was not much fun to be around anymore. I was creating an atmosphere of stress, and it seemed like I cared more about packages than people.

I thought about it, and she was absolutely right. I apologized and asked her to reconsider her resignation. Thankfully, she accepted my apology and decided to stay. In fact, she advanced into other roles in the years that followed and eventually completed a tremendous career with UPS.

I needed to get my priorities back on track, which meant taking better care of *myself*. I knew I was doing a terrible job in that department, and it was undermining my ability to lead. From that day on, self-leadership became my top priority.

Consider how you manage your own time and how you handle the inevitable changes that bring challenges, excitement—and yes, even grief and anguish—into your life. *Are you always two steps behind instead of one step ahead? What about advances in your field and all the innovations that seem to come along almost daily? Are you up-to-date with the latest technology and best business practices? How are you doing with your health?*

Make Deadlines a Key Part
of Your Planning Process

Students study harder and are better at blocking out distractions when a final exam is looming. Moms-to-be decorate nurseries to beat the due date of a coming baby. Details for a wedding begin to look like an oncoming freight train for those preparing for the big day.

Business is no different from these other areas of life. Make deadlines a key part of your planning process. *Projects that have deadlines get done.*

When you take the time it takes, it takes less time. The fewer things you do, the more things you accomplish. There are numerous time-management systems available. Use one that works for you. Mine is just one of many:

Step 1: Determine Priorities Every Day

You already know what your priorities should be. Chances are, however, you might have trouble concentrating your time and energy on the *right* activities each day.

Avoid engaging in a battle of *the trivial many against the vital few.* Instead, set aside a few minutes each day to decide what projects and tasks are a priority, and, more important, which ones are not. Prioritize those tasks based upon your goals, and then attack them one by one, in order. As important things pop up, add them to your daily list. Check off items as they are completed. Don't try to keep all of the items on your to-do list in your head; write them down.

Step 2: Take Time Every Week to Chart a Schedule

Withdraw from your normal routine for a couple of hours and plan the upcoming week. Try some different days and times until you find the one that works best for you. A disciplined approach to managing time will keep you focused and build momentum in your favor. When you take the time to set clear targets and chart a well-defined schedule, you will become much more consistent. Don't make it up as you go along.

Step 3: Monitor Your Plan Monthly

Decide daily (Step 1) and take time weekly (Step 2), but make sure you also monitor monthly. A good rule of thumb is that 10 percent of your time at work should be dedicated to planning and the other 90 percent to working the plan.

If you invest a percentage of your time in planning, you will accomplish far more than people who spend little or no time planning and who instead fly by the seat of their pants.

You may be thinking, "There is no way I have that much time to sit around planning." Maybe there is a reason you don't have the time. *Could it be that you have no time because you have no plan?* Planning is not "sitting around." The truth is, planning is possibly the hardest work you will do. It is surely among the most important.

Step 4: Meet Yearly with Staff outside the Office

Consider going on a retreat with your staff at least once a year with a set agenda that includes but is not limited to planning and goal setting. For years, I used to think pulling away like this was a waste of time and money. That was before I did it.

Once I tried this approach, I realized my management team became more closely aligned and a lot more focused when they were away from their routine work environment and all of the distractions that go with it. One rule: No interruptions, human or electronic.

How *You* Can Deliver

- Figure out your *It*—the one thing you were born to do.
- Learn to manage yourself before you begin managing others.
- Be only and exactly who you are. Don't try to be someone else.
- Set an example with a positive attitude and people will follow your lead.
- Manage your time and become an expert at planning.
- Remember that when you take the time it takes, it takes less time.

CHAPTER 5

Targeting the Most Critical Information

W hen I was in the fourth grade, my teacher, Mrs. Cesped, taught us that by asking *What? Who? How? Why?* we could discover just about anything we wanted to know. Although I didn't know it at the time, Mrs. Cesped was teaching us to think like leaders and to grasp the importance of focusing on the critical information we needed to make the best possible decisions.

When you make it a habit to ask your management team about the things that really matter—questions that get to the heart of the work they do—something very interesting starts to occur. It makes them dig deeper into the details of their jobs and discover things that need attention. Asking questions that target critical information sends a signal to them that they are personally responsible to know every minute detail of their job and they will be accountable for their performance.

Ask Questions That Are Provocative Probes

Steve Gordon, a division manager for UPS, had an opening for a manager's position in his hub. As it turned out, two supervisors on his team were qualified for the position and had roughly equal experience. However, one had a few more years with the company than the other.

After an extensive interview process, Steve decided to offer the position to the person who had fewer years. She accepted. The other supervisor wasn't too happy about the decision and asked Steve for a meeting to ask why he was passed over in favor of a supervisor with less time in the company.

Steve decided the best way to answer this question was to ask a few questions of his own. Therefore, he asked about the volume that had been processed in the hub the previous night. The supervisor said he would check, and a few minutes later returned and reported that the volume was about normal and there were no known problems.

Steve then asked how many packages there were and whether they were dispatched on time. The supervisor left once again; and when he returned, he told Steve "Approximately 120,000, and they were dispatched on time."

Steve continued to ask questions, and the employee continued to excuse himself and later return with the answer.

Finally, Steve completed his round of questioning and asked the supervisor to sit in the office next to his, door ajar, and to listen to the conversation he was about to have with the newly promoted manager.

When the newly promoted manager arrived in his office, Steve asked her to tell him about the volume that had been processed in the hub the previous night. She said, "122,479 packages were processed with no problems, and the operation closed at 3:22 a.m. Of that total, 121,368 were ground packages and 1,111 were air. All outbound volume departed on time, and the pre-load was completed at 6:45 a.m. The delivery drivers were dispatched on schedule, with one package car taken out of service at 9:00 a.m. due to a flat tire. The tire was replaced, and the car was back on the road by 9:30 a.m."

Steve thanked her and she left his office. He then asked the supervisor who was passed over for the promotion to come back into his office. Without any prompting from Steve, he said he had heard the whole conversation and understood why she had received the promotion and he had not.

Whenever you ask your managers questions about *their* operations, they will in turn ask *their* people the same questions. Once this leadership trait becomes a habit, dominoes will fall and this virtual circle of accountability will raise everyone's game, along with the bottom line.

Leaders need to know what is going on inside their operations, and the best ones know the key facts off the top of their heads. They've got the answers when asked.

Let's look closely at how you can leverage the power of Mrs. Cesped's four questions—the *What*, the *Who*, the *How*, and the *Why*.

The *What*

It is impossible to hit a target if you don't know what it is. A team that has not identified *what* they are trying to do will fail. Therefore, determining the *what* must be one of your top responsibilities.

Each member of your team has different strengths and unique abilities. Getting them to operate as a coordinated unit—all moving in the same direction and toward the same goal—is the job of the leader. If they are not crystal clear about *what* they are sup-posed to be doing, it is going to be difficult and most likely im-possible to achieve your organization's objectives.

An old term used by motorcyclists, *target fixation*, means that wherever you look while riding a motorcycle, the bike will follow. In other words, you shouldn't look at the guardrail when you go into a curve or that's where you'll end up.

This type of *misdirected* focus can get you into real trouble, both on the road and in your life.

What Target Fixation Looks Like

When Monica was five years old, her uncle took her to a large empty parking lot to teach her how to ride her new bicycle. The lot had plenty of room and no obstacles except for one gigantic light pole on the far side of the lot.

As her uncle steadied the bike and Monica began pedaling, she gained her balance and he knew it was safe to let go. All of a sudden, though, she looked up at the light pole on the far side of the parking lot and began screaming, "I'm gonna hit the pole! I'm gonna hit the pole!" Her uncle shouted, "No, you're not! Just turn the handle bars." But Monica kept her focus locked onto the light pole and kept pedaling.

Guess what? She hit the pole.

Instead of focusing on the fact that she was actually riding her bike and had total control of the situation, Monica couldn't stop looking at the pole. If she had switched her target fixation from the pole to where she wanted to go, she wouldn't have ended up flat on the pavement.

Keep yourself and your people focused on the right things. Your answer to the *what* is your vision for the team. When you clearly communicate your vision, your people will be inspired to concentrate on the right things and you and your company won't end up in the ditch. Yielding to the natural temptation to focus on the "poles" that are in your way—the wrong *whats*—is a big mistake. If you concentrate on the wrong issues, or simply fixate on your problems, they will consume you.

Have the vision to see beyond your circumstances, problems, and emotions, and focus on the right targets. When you have the right *who*, the *what* is going to get done.

The *Who*

Being a successful leader also demands that you figure out the *who*. The people who work for you are the ones who will make the *what* happen.

To learn about your people, you must get to know them personally, not just their names and job responsibilities. Ask them to share their viewpoints, concerns, personal goals, and dreams, as my trainer Fred did with me on my first day with UPS.

When the people on your team believe that you value them as individuals, that you care about what they think, they will be excited to be part of your team. People who know that they matter and are convinced they are appreciated will work harder and add more value to the team.

By asking questions about your team's goals (the *what*) and discovering the details about each person on the team (the *who*), you will have laid the foundation for deciding the correct course of action (the *how*).

The *How*

We live in a cut-and-paste world of ideas. A tried-and-true business strategy with proven results in other companies can be very tempting to copy. Remember, though, there is no guarantee that what works well for another company will work for you.

There are endless options for answering the *how*, but the best answer is usually the one that is doable. Focus on how to become better at what you already do and then be ready to make the inevitable necessary changes along the way.

> Once when his staff was debating the best way to fend off the competition, Chick-fil-A's founder S. Truett Cathy pounded his fist on a conference room table and flatly told his staff, "If we get better, our customers will demand we get bigger!"
>
> Mr. Cathy was right. It is a basic truth and operating principle in business: change is inevitable; growth is optional.

The most effective leaders know every aspect of their business and pursue the ever-changing demands of their customers. Get your team to understand this unavoidable reality well and watch all those little details like a hawk. Constantly study your industry while keeping a close eye on every part of your business.

You don't want surprises, and you need to have practical options for almost every possible scenario. Surround yourself with experienced and motivated people who stay ahead of the game. That will be your *how*.

The *Why*

What, who, and *how* are natural questions for anyone who is trying to set the direction for an organization. However, the most important question might be the *why*.

Think about how leaders inspire people to action. They start by telling them *why* they do what they do and lay out a compelling vision for the future. When people are moved to follow a vision, they are not so much buying into *what* you want to accomplish as they are agreeing with *why* you want to do it. Leaders need to inspire their teams to see opportunities that others don't and to effectively communicate how they are going to reach the summit together.

To enhance service offerings and grow market share in a short time, at one point UPS acquired twenty-six different companies. All were good organizations with their own histories and cultures. However, they were set in their ways of doing business.

Their inflexibility became a challenge for our leadership team, as we tried to integrate them into the UPS culture and the way we did business. During the early stages of this process, some troubling internal attitudes and external friction surfaced, including a fracturing brand identity. We began to look like several different companies—confusing both employees and customers.

The leadership or owners of the companies we purchased were happy to remain separate and distinct from one another, but we needed to meld the pieces together with great skill and care. There was a lot at stake. Our CEO at the time, Mike Eskew, took the reins and communicated with our new partners exactly why we needed to have just *one* UPS. The message was clear: UPS—one company, one vision, one brand.

We formed teams that were driven solely by careful attention to our shared goal: to relaunch the UPS brand, along with a new corporate logo, better setting the course for the future. After a lot of hard work by people from UPS and representatives from the acquired companies, eventually everyone got on the same page and moved forward together.

The mission was accomplished: one company, one vision, one brand. That happened because everyone knew *why* they were doing what they did: to create one UPS.

Ready, Aim, Fire
Let's put all four questions together into steps that you can apply in your own business.

1. Identify *what* you are supposed to accomplish (*your mission and goals*).

2. Then determine *how* you are going to do it (*your strategy*).
3. Know *who* is going to do it (*your team*).
4. Understand *why* you are doing what you are doing (*your vision*).

When the answers to these questions are all working together in harmony, your organization will be in alignment.

Take a Ready, Aim, Fire Approach

The best way to consistently hit the target is to take a *Ready-Aim-Fire* approach and assess what happens by gathering relevant information and analyzing results.

Step 1: Identify Your Target

Before you start firing at your target, do your homework. Identify the specific target and then choose the appropriate "weapon." Identify your target—hone your vision—by asking, "What am I trying to accomplish and why?" Your weapon and ammunition are your resources. Assess readiness by asking whether you have the right team with the right skills and all the means necessary to accomplish the vision you have spelled out.

Step 2: Aim Your Resources

Verify your goals (your *what*), define a strategy (your *how*), and then point your weapon at the target.

Step 3: Fire

It is time to pull the trigger.

Firearms instructors say, "You can't miss fast enough to win," which means accuracy is more important than speed in shooting. The same principle is true for designing the right strategy. If you take the time to prepare properly at the outset, the odds of hitting your target go way up.

Unsuccessful leaders use the *Ready, Fire, Aim* approach and consistently miss the target. Successful leaders practice Ready, Aim, Fire. Of course, another option might be to "shoot first and call whatever you hit the target."

There is actually a valid point in that claim. If you aim and get close, but don't always hit the bull's-eye, is that necessarily a bad thing? Maybe not. It's likely that the more you shoot using the right techniques, the better you will get.

One thing is certain: If you don't take a shot, you will *never* hit any target, much less the bull's-eye!

Sometimes, however, the actual target is not what everyone thinks it is.

Be Sure to Clearly Communicate Your Target

Innovator Tom Wujec references a survey of 50,000 CEOs who were asked if their vision had been clearly communicated and was being executed effectively. Not surprisingly, 80 percent answered that they believed it was. However, only 20 percent of the team members of those same 50,000 CEOs believed the vision was both clear and being carried out.[9]

That is quite a gap. *So how do you close a gap like that?*

You do it by asking your coworkers many questions and seeking their honest feedback. *What are they thinking, hearing, and understanding?* Pursue the truth to get everyone connected and moving in the same direction. It is essential to understand each team member's point of view and to check frequently that the understanding is mutual. Identify those gaps in your organization and eliminate them as soon as possible.

Don't just communicate—connect the dots! Think about all those emails, messages, texts, and memos you generate. *Have you closed the loop to get the desired result?* Or, as we saw with the CEO

Leaders Focus on the Big Picture

Too often, managers get caught up believing that the solution to a problem is filling out endless forms or performing numerous internal processes. Instead of helping, these procedures unnecessarily burden those people responsible for the big picture: delivering what customers have paid for.

I used to ask my managers to bring one or two reports to each staff meeting that could be condensed or even eliminated. Staff then worked with the operators to analyze them and discuss their findings at the next meeting.

It was amazing to me how many reports and forms we eliminated as a direct result of this simple process. Of course, this efficiency-driven focus saved staff and operators time, and they all loved doing away with unnecessary paperwork.

We had to be careful not to have so many procedures that people were overwhelmed to the point of burnout. Often those procedures exist just because *that's the way it's always been*. Leaders who care about their team members need to find ways to make their jobs easier and more effective. This involves getting rid of the anchors around the necks of productivity.

---

study, *have you just put out a ton of information, hoping that something will stick?*

All the information that goes out from you and your staff and colleagues in a given month would probably fill a small truck.

How *You* Can Deliver

- Ask questions and listen closely until you are satisfied your group is aligned with your vision.
- Once you have selected your *what*, focus on the *who*, *how*, and *why*.
- Don't just communicate. Connect the dots.
- Review current practices to determine what can be improved and what can be eliminated.
- Question the purpose of each report. If you don't need it, get rid of it.

CHAPTER 6

Cultivating the X Factor

X Factor (n): *Critical characteristics for effective leadership*

G reat leaders understand that *every single person makes the company what it is.* To build a championship team, hire, develop, and promote people with diverse strengths and then trust them to do their jobs.

This is what leads to $1 + 1 + 1 = 5$. That's the kind of arithmetic that makes a leader's job exhilarating and fun and the accountants and stockholders very happy, too!

It's one thing to build a championship-caliber team

To build a championship team, hire, develop, and promote people with diverse strengths and then trust them to do their jobs.

when you get to handpick from a pool of experienced and talented people. It can be an entirely different scenario when you take over an established organization where, more often than not, you get what you get. The business world is not like the NFL draft, where you choose from a long list of the best players on earth.

X Factor 1: The Ability to Match People and Jobs

You've got to establish bridges of trust with your people while learning each person's strengths—and weaknesses. The ability to match the right individual to the right job is one of those uncanny abilities that X factor leaders can do better than anyone else. The best leaders execute the selection-and-assignment process with surgical precision.

Helping your people succeed requires placing them in positions that are the right fit. However, rotating people through a number of functions can bring tremendous value to the team and prepares them for more responsibility as they progress through their careers.

For example, former UPS Chairman and CEO Oz Nelson started as a part-time car washer. After working as a package car driver, he worked his way through the ranks and eventually became the corporate business development manager. Later, he was promoted to chief financial officer prior to becoming chairman of the board and chief executive officer of the company.

So, just how do you surround yourself with great people?

Pick Good People, Train Them Well, Then Step Back

One measure of your success is how much you build up others and prepare them for greater responsibility. When you build up others, you build up yourself. Developing people and watching them grow, take on more responsibility, and succeed will be one of your most rewarding experiences as a leader.

Teddy Roosevelt once said, "The best executive is one who has sense enough to pick good people to do what he wants done, and self-restraint enough to keep from meddling with them while they do it." Unfortunately, many leaders like to meddle and they end up making decisions their people could and should make.

When you need to hire new employees or promote existing ones, first choose the right people. And who are the right people? They are those who have similar values as your organization and a history of high integrity and a strong work ethic. After hiring them, ensure they receive the proper training, clearly communicate your expectations, and then step back and let them do their job.

As you get to know your people better, you will identify the great ones, the good ones, and the ones who need a little help. The last thing you want is to start over with new people and lose all the institutional knowledge and experience that seasoned employees have accumulated. Although turnover is sometimes necessary, and even a good thing, it can be disruptive and expensive.

Learn to observe and evaluate, and resist the urge to make impulsive decisions about personnel changes. Be patient and carefully consider your options before taking action. You will thank yourself later on.

Under enormous pressure, I learned an important lesson about matching the right person to a critical project. Late one afternoon while working in my office in San Francisco, I was notified we had to move out of one of the largest buildings in the district. Even more disturbing was the news that we had to evacuate the building within six months.

We had already made plans to replace the facility in the next year and a half. But on this particular day, our attorneys discovered that the fine print in an amendment to the lease agreement gave the landlord the right to evict tenants with only a six-month notice. Overnight, the timeline for our well-thought-out relocation plan shrank from eighteen months to six.

Recognize When the "Right" Person Is Wrong for the Job

Fortunately, the construction of our new building was well underway; but if we were going to move in ahead of schedule, we needed to complete the move twelve months sooner than planned. In addition, creating an operating plan to relocate more than three hundred employees in such a short time frame was a massive undertaking for us.

With no time to waste, I assigned one of our best industrial engineers to head up the project. I thought he was the perfect person for the job. He was one of the smartest people in the district and had years of experience at UPS. I gave him free rein to use whatever resources he needed to get the job done.

Much to my surprise, it soon became clear the project was falling behind schedule under his leadership. He turned out to be such a perfectionist that he focused on every minute detail himself, rather than delegating and holding his team accountable for meeting critical deadlines. He lacked a sense of urgency and wasted valuable time as he tried to put every aspect of the job under a microscope.

Before stepping in directly, I asked several staff-level managers to help him out, but we just couldn't get his fire lit. With critical deadlines approaching, I had no choice but to take him off the project.

Be Willing to Take a Chance

I took a chance and gave the assignment to an operations manager named Megan. She had no experience in projects like this, but she had a wealth of knowledge about operations and a reputation for getting things done. Well-respected by her peers, she was a team builder who didn't hesitate to hold people accountable for their performance.

Megan was fearless and had what it took: initiative, passion, courage, and the attitude to do whatever was needed to get the job done. Once I put her in charge, she took off like a bullet train to get the project back on track and into the station on time. Sparks flew and urgency was in the air and that is exactly what I was hoping to see.

Neither Megan nor I accepted 90 percent as good enough, but we both realized that 98 percent and on time was better than 100 percent and late. She might have lacked the technical background but more than made up for it with her leadership skills and desire to succeed. Because of her passion and relentless drive to get the job done, the new building opened right on schedule, and the transition plan for relocation was executed flawlessly. Megan received a well-deserved promotion less than a year later.

At first, the industrial engineer seemed to be the logical person to head the effort, especially compared to someone who had no experience in projects of this magnitude. However, fielding our best manager in this case meant putting the person with the best fit of specific competencies in charge.

X Factor 2: The Ability to Remove the Fog

To ensure that you clearly communicate with the members of your team, use this four-step approach.

Step 1: Clearly State Your Expectations and Then Follow Up

This sounds obvious, but you would be surprised how many leaders just assume their team knows what to do. Assuming anything in a leadership role is a *major* mistake.

There is nothing more frustrating for motivated people than not knowing exactly what is expected of them. Be clear by being specific and then *follow up* (the two magic words) to ensure everyone truly understands what you want them to do.

Continue to recast the vision, over and over. Remove all of the fog and, if necessary, put your expectations in writing. Keep it simple and direct.

To ensure you've communicated your expectations, state them in the following terms:
- The result you want
- The standards the result must meet
- The deadline (whether it's flexible or in concrete)
- The budget
- The resources available
- Any constraints (sacred cows to avoid)
- When and how to report progress
- How their performance will be measured
- That you are available to help

Step 2: Translate Your Expectations into Deliverables

Deliverables are the expected results, not to be confused with the activities that lead to the end product. For example, if you order a pizza for delivery, you place your order and wait for the driver to bring exactly what you ordered to your house. You don't tell them how to make the pizza or how to drive the delivery vehicle.

It's one thing to say, "I expect you to hit your goals for the month." It's another thing altogether to tell your team every little detail of *how* to do it. You have placed these folks in their positions *because they know how to do it.* Once you have let your team know what they need to deliver and when it needs to arrive, get out of the way.

Step 3: Hold People Accountable

Everyone needs accountability—you included. It's amazing how much performance improves when managers are around. Remember—what gets inspected gets done.

If you don't follow through with both inspections and acknowledgments, it is easy for people to think that what they're doing isn't important. If assignments are not important enough for the person in charge to check on them, then the quality of the work will decline and the results will fall short of the standards you expected.

Step 4: Check Your Own Progress Regularly

You may feel as though you have the right to tell people what to do, but having that right doesn't guarantee you are actually influencing anyone. *The gap between a leader's expectations and a follower's actions is usually more about their relationship than it is about matters of substance.* If you sense a gap, it might be time to do some relational fence mending.

X Factor 3: The Ability to Inspire and Go Higher

The best leaders are great encouragers, and they inspire their team to achieve more than they ever thought possible. Performance without acknowledgment kills morale. If all you ever do is state expectations and measure performance, be ready to lead a lifeless team.

Show Your Appreciation

You can show your appreciation to employees with a simple, heartfelt "Thank you," or a timely "Good job." This costs you nothing. Failing to acknowledge others with praise might cost you more than you can measure.

Your skill in acknowledging people for a job well done can be one of your greatest assets. An encouraging word from you can sustain an employee for weeks, and a *handwritten* thank-you note will be appreciated and often cherished, as they realize that you noticed—and it was important enough that you took the time to write a personal note.

I always kept a stack of thank-you notes on my desk. They were a constant reminder to thank people for their good work. Of course, there are many ways to inspire people and not all of them are pleasant. As you will soon see, one man's trash can be the source of another man's treasure.

Specify the Reason for an Acknowledgment

Whenever you recognize someone for a job well done, follow it with clear and specific details as to why you think they deserved to be acknowledged. For example: "Great job, Jennifer. Your quick and accurate information leading to the diagnosis of the problem last weekend provided the exact data that we needed to close that order. Keep up the great work! I really appreciate what you do."

X Factor 4: The Ability to Be Creative

Increasing package volume was not easy in the early days of UPS operations in Germany. Our business development people worked hard, but were making little progress. They implemented all the tried-and-true methods that were available to them, but they were running out of ideas and leads.

Sales leads produce business: it's that simple. Without sales leads, nothing happens, and that is what we faced. Our sales force was frustrated and running out of steam.

At that time, we had two districts, north and south, which covered the entire country. The other district manager and I decided to have a joint meeting with all of our business development people, who numbered more than one hundred. The goal of the meeting was to reenergize our team by collaborating, learning from each other, and talking about what was and wasn't working.

The conference setting was a typical one. To add importance, we invited Jim McLaughlin, our corporate president, to attend the meeting.

The day-and-a-half-long session went pretty much as we expected, and we had anticipated that Jim would give everyone in attendance some inspirational closing remarks. We were wrong.

Jim is a pull-no-punches, say-it-like-it-is kind of guy. He stood up at the end of the meeting and sternly announced: "Extend your hotel rooms for another night. I want every one of you to meet me in front of the hotel in one hour. Wear old clothes if you have them. Each of you needs to bring a knife, a pair of scissors, or whatever you can find that cuts."

Exactly one hour later, more than one hundred UPS people were standing in front of the hotel, each one holding some kind of cutting instrument.

Jim said, "Follow me" and took off walking down the main street of the little village on the Baltic Sea. It looked like some sort of parade, as local people began lining the sidewalks in amazement. No one, including me, had any idea what was going on.

Suddenly our little parade turned the corner and we found ourselves in an alley that ran for kilometers behind the shops and stores. Jim explained our mission, which was to last well into the night.

"Everyone divide up into teams of two—you will take turns," he instructed. "One of you will get into the dumpster behind each store and remove every single box. Then the two of you will cut the shipping and receiving label from each of those boxes. When that is completed, you are to go across the street and do the same thing—and continue until every last dumpster in this city has been searched."

With that, we embarked on our assigned task. Why we didn't end up in jail is beyond me.

When some of the merchants asked us if we had lost our minds—wanting to know what the heck we were doing—we just told them the truth. "We are UPS salespeople, and we want the labels from the boxes that you are throwing out for sales leads." They seemed to accept the explanation, and into the night we worked. Jim stayed on-scene to ensure the operation went as planned.

After we finished digging through the dumpsters, Jim instructed everyone to return to the conference room with all of the labels we had collected. The fruits of our work were stacks of torn and dirty labels, and our marathon sorting session lasted the rest of the night. Soon people began to realize that what they had in front of them was gold nuggets. They were leads—*solid* leads, because they were from real shippers and real receivers.

When the Usual Methods Don't Work, Find New Ones

Jim had seen a better way to get the job done. When usual methods were not working, he got creative. His approach was simple and direct. He made us get our hands dirty and pan for gold.

Times have changed, of course, and no one at UPS would dare suggest anything like dumpster diving today. But hundreds of leads came from those dirty old boxes mixed in with the other garbage. Within a few weeks, our sales staff had contacted all the companies found on those labels.

Before we knew it, our delivery centers had packages coming out of their ears. The leads from those dumpsters brought us many new customers and cars full of new packages.

Did a Sugar Cube Save UPS Germany?

The momentum from that day snowballed. We made it a country-wide campaign that involved all employees. It became very competitive and turned into a contest where employees and even their families were rewarded for every lead that turned into a new customer.

I remember handing a manager a paper-wrapped sugar cube for his coffee at breakfast one morning and he asked me what it was.

"It's a sugar cube," I replied, wondering if he had asked a trick question.

The manager said, "No, it's not—look!"

He showed me the wrapper. On it was printed the manufacturer's name, address, and phone number. He proudly told everyone at the table the object he was holding in his hand wasn't a *sugar cube*, it was a *lead*. Darned if that sugar cube lead didn't end up becoming one of UPS's largest customers in Germany.

More than thirty years after that infamous dumpster-diving event, I attended a regional meeting in Germany. During the

---

HOW LEADERSHIP LOOKS FROM HERE

Leaders Guide Their Teams to Higher Levels

A worthwhile personal goal for any leader should be to *help people become better than you* and guide them to higher levels in the company. As I did this, I surrounded myself with great people and delegation took on a new meaning. I had to learn to trust my staff with the *whats* and turn them loose on the *hows*.

Remove the fog about what everyone is doing. Leaders are responsible for making expectations and deliverables unmistakably clear and then holding their people accountable to meet them. Great leaders assume nothing.

When the old ways don't work, *quit hitting the same wall and get creative*. Jim McLaughlin was a leader with that elusive X factor. He led us to an unexpected place via an alleyway of dumpsters in a village on the Baltic Sea.

---

meeting, I received a gift presented in a large, nicely wrapped box. I opened the box, and inside was one little sugar cube. It, not me, got a standing ovation as I held it up for everyone to see.

How *You* Can Deliver

- The sum is greater than the whole when you hire, develop, and trust your people.
- Your team will succeed when you put the right people in the right jobs.
- Measure your own personal success by how well your people develop and grow.
- Find those who need help, then provide it.
- Look deep, be creative, take a chance to find the way to get the job done—find your "Megan."

- Remove fog by stating expectations clearly in terms of deliverables and follow up by inspecting frequently.
- Acknowledge good performance—quickly and specifically. Make a habit of finding people who are doing the right things.
- Keep thank-you notes on your desk and use them often.
- Replace excuses with solutions.

CHAPTER 7

Maintaining an Ethical Environment

Be Alert to Skewing

In my teenage years working on a ranch, part of my job was to clean out the barn twice a day. It was filled with horses, hogs, a few head of cattle, and way too many chickens. The temperature inside the barn was normally above 80 degrees. During my first few days on the job, I could stand the smell for only a few minutes before I had to rush outside and gasp for fresh air. With each passing day, however, I found I could hang in there for longer and longer periods of time.

Each day I thought the smell was a little less overwhelming; but, in fact, the smell had not changed at all. My sense of smell had simply become skewed. In business, skewing occurs when people try to make their performance look better than it really is. In most cases, this means they are manipulating the numbers or taking shortcuts that violate company policy or its code of ethics. In some circles, this is known as "making bad numbers look good." Some people may try to justify it and even convince themselves that it is part of doing business. After a while, that skewed picture becomes their reality.

Skewing happens in other ways, too. How many times have you walked into a business that was disorganized or dirty or witnessed employees giving poor service to customers? In such organizations, sloppy appearance, poor customer service, and even inappropriate behaviors have become not only tolerated, they have slowly become the norm.

Over time, if management continues to neglect such critical warning signs, employees will become numb to the downward slide. When this happens, that strong barn smell becomes imperceptible to those living in the barn, but your customers and others will certainly notice.

All employees, regardless of position, need to be honest and do the right things. Occasionally, a few people convince themselves and those around them that a little fudging here and there is not so bad, and it lures them into trading their ethics for personal gain. Others may mistakenly believe that as long as their chosen course of action is within the confines of the law, they have done nothing wrong. That view disregards ethical boundaries and is simply not true. Just because it isn't illegal doesn't make it right or just.

Letting your senses adapt to what's around you may not be such a big deal when you are shoveling manure, but it's a huge deal when you are trying to create a healthy and productive work environment for your people. Perhaps, over a long time, you have allowed some things to become skewed in your organization. Maybe it was even that way when you got there. Whatever the case may be, it's your job to right the ship.

Assess yourself and your team. Do a "smell test" occasionally. Take the time to ask yourself, "Am I getting used to the smell around here?" If something doesn't smell right, take immediate action and find the source of this unpleasant odor.

Set the Standard and Remain Above Reproach

It is the responsibility of the organization's leadership to create a culture based on integrity by setting the standard and remaining above reproach at all times.

Leaders are vulnerable; the higher your position, the more vulnerable you become. This means that you must do everything you can to stay away from situations where your character could be called into question. Great leaders never give anyone a reason to question their motives or their morals and they remain steadfast in their belief that the right way to do things will always be the right way to do things.

Having a clear conscience is powerful. It allows you to be more confident as a leader because there are no invisible burdens weighing you down. It may sound trivial; however, I think this may be the most important thing you can take away from this book.

Recognize When Independent Counsel May Be Helpful

If you have forged strong bonds with your people and created a climate of open and honest communication, they will let you know when something isn't right. Whenever your employees have been conditioned to breathe the same exhaust you are breathing, you may want to get assistance from outside professionals. You might think you cannot afford a consultant, but the truth may be just the opposite. Your organization might be in a bad place because you failed to get independent and unbiased counsel.

Outsiders don't stand inside your barn all day and will thus be able to quickly detect "that smell." A fresh perspective may be just what the doctor ordered.

Be Someone Your Team Can Trust

In a survey sponsored by Fast Company, the International Institute for Management Development, and Egon Zehnder International, 95 percent of employees replied "yes" or "absolutely" when asked the question: "Do the ethics of the CEO play a meaningful role in the way business gets done?" This echoes the *U.S. News & World Report*/Harvard University study cited in chapter 3 and confirms the overwhelming desire among employees for their leader to have integrity above all other traits.

Your people will notice if you start work late, take long lunches, and leave early. They will notice if you cut corners, waste time, fail to do meaningful work, or fudge here and there. If people are going to follow you, they want assurance that they can trust you. If they cannot, they will back away. Warren Buffett once said, "It takes 20 years to build a reputation and five minutes to ruin it. If you think about that, you'll do things differently." If Warren said it, that's good enough for me.

Perform Regular Team Checkups

Perform regular checkups on your team, assessing the value of each member and his or her contributions (or lack thereof). These are indicators of your team's vital statistics:

- Which team members contribute the most to ensuring that the business is successful?
- Who is negatively affecting your team and inhibiting progress?
- Who—or what—is slowing things down?
- Who has fallen into a rut?
- Who is pulling their coworkers off track?
- Who on your team is keeping a low profile—hoping you won't notice their lack of accomplishments?

Believe me, in hectic business environments there can be lots of places to hide.

Identify Who's Rocking the Boat

When everyone is rowing in the same direction, there's practically nothing that can keep you from winning the race. However, sometimes you will have people who would rather rock the boat than help you move it forward (and almost every organization has them). You cannot allow these individuals to undermine your influence and impede the team's progress. It is your job to praise the rowers and tell the rockers to walk the plank.

Ensure That Your Team's Skills Don't Get Rusty

People can have all the talent, skill, and experience in the world and still not perform up to their potential. *Why?* Rust never sleeps.

Recognize when a member of your team is getting rusty or even burned out. If other approaches aren't working, you may want to try a more oblique approach. Get them involved with current training opportunities. Assign them to jobs and extra duties that will ensure their skills are constantly being applied and improved. Reenergize them with tasks that will put them in the limelight and help rekindle their enthusiasm. It's possible there's something going on in their personal life you're unaware of that is weighing them down. Find out what buttons need pushing to motivate them to get back in the game.

Challenge Team Members When They're Coasting

Are some of your team members just going through the motions? Muscle memory isn't all that bad for routine tasks: it's how we play a musical instrument, hit a golf ball, or drive a car. But, in a business setting, people often put their real talents on autopilot and coast, surviving rather than thriving, by innovating and pushing themselves to higher levels of performance.

If someone on your team is coasting, they are hurting the entire team's progress and restricting their own growth as well. Call them on it and challenge them to flip the switch, reengage, and push themselves out of the comfortable and familiar.

And just how do you do that?

Take a step back and look at the big picture with these questions:

- Does my company have the right programs in place to prevent burnout?
- Do I rotate people in and out of jobs?
- Do I send them to workshops or special training?
- Are my recognition programs working?
- Are my supervisors making frequent contacts with their people?
- Do I have an open-door policy?
- Are my people involved and engaged?
- Do I have frequent group meetings to keep them informed?

Clear communication, and lots of it, cures many things. Often, just a one-on-one talk expressing your concern is all that is needed.

Even a simple thing can have an impact, like having someone lead employees in stretching exercises before work.

Take Steps to Keep Team Members Involved

At the suggestion of our safety committee in one of our larger hubs, we hung a traffic light from the ceiling just inside the main entry door. If the light was green, the hub employees were on a run with no lost-time injuries. If it turned red, everyone was alerted that an injury had occurred. Whenever this happened, we would hold a group meeting with all employees under the stoplight as it flashed red. We reviewed the injury in greater detail, including reenacting exactly how it happened, to remind folks of unsafe acts or unsafe conditions. Then the safety committee, a team composed of part-time hourly employees, gave additional training on that specific injury. At the end of the shift, the light switched back to green and the run started anew.

When people arrived at work to start their shifts, the first thing they did was look up at the light. It was a remarkably simple thing, but it brought focus to the many safety programs we had in place. We emphasized working safely by following safe work habits above anything else, and no one wanted to make the red light come on. We were proud of the fact that in a building with more than 1,000 employees, the light stayed green for over two years straight, setting the pace for the entire company. Many awards were handed out under that green light along the way.

Don't Deceive Your Leaders, Even If You Have to Offend Them

If you were driving down the road and saw a sign that said, "Bridge Out Ahead" or "Dead End," you would change course, right? Those kinds of warning signs appear in organizations as well. Whenever they're brought to your attention, listen; they may help you avoid a catastrophe.

It's easier to do well if people feel free to speak up when they see their leader heading toward the ditch. Once, when I was a district manager, I could easily have ended up in the ditch.

One of the hardest things I ever had to do was cause the termination of a colleague who, at the time, was one of my closest friends. It was brought to my attention that he had not only violated policy, but his actions had put the company in a very difficult situation that could have brought serious consequences. When I talked to him and he confirmed what I had discovered was true, I was heartbroken.

HOW LEADERSHIP LOOKS FROM HERE

Leaders Act with Integrity

I learned that a leader must make the hard decisions and do what is right for the team every single time, *even* when it is unpopular. When all the talk has been exhausted, leadership is a duty-based, disciplined mentality that exists independent of one's own whims and preferences. It is a manner of thinking vastly different from the one I had in those days when I was concerned primarily with doing my job and my job alone. The view changed radically as I assumed increasing levels of responsibility for the well-being of the entire international organization.

I told him he needed to talk to the region manager. He told me he couldn't and wouldn't, and I honestly understood why. So, I did what had to be done. I reported my friend to his manager and he was fired the next morning.

Effective leaders surround themselves with loyal and trustworthy people who have the courage to say it like it is, even if their words hit sensitive topics or are painful to hear. Your best managers are those who know of problems and then fearlessly bring them to your attention.

Some may say they don't want to throw their teammates under the bus, but the truth is they knowingly do the team and the company a serious disservice by not promptly reporting concerns so they can be addressed. That is part of leadership integrity. You want people who have your back and have the courage to tell you about that "bridge out" ahead.

Be Prepared to Perform in a Crisis

When asked how he became a war hero, President John F. Kennedy said, "They sank my boat."[10] A crisis can blow you out of the water and make you lose sight of your objectives completely. It doesn't have to be that way. A crisis can actually sharpen your focus, but only if you maintain concentration and perspective.

When others lose their will, leaders strengthen their resolve to overcome and succeed. When you feel like your boat is sinking, don't panic. View every crisis as an opportunity. A crisis can be a turning point in your career. Like JFK, be prepared to perform under pressure.

View every crisis as an opportunity.

Plans change, employees leave, and players get injured. People get sick and friends move across the country. Just when we think we can relax and settle in, our kids rebel, or the boss says, "I have bad news." The list never ends; in time, circumstances will eventually go against you.

When you find yourself facing a crisis and under the gun, you may find this three-step approach to crisis management helpful.

Step 1: Know Your Options
Recognize your options in crisis management, risk analysis, and conflict resolution. Consider a variety of what-if scenarios and then prepare for those potential crises by thinking through the best reactions under a variety of different conditions. For example: What if half of our Seattle-to-Alaska package car cavalry had broken down and needed towing on the ALCAN Highway?

In this way, when things go bad, your team will be ready to go the second it's needed.

Step 2: Expect the Unexpected
Anticipating what can and will go wrong can keep you calm and focused in a storm when a sudden crisis occurs. In law

enforcement, this is called *cognitive dominance*—the mental state of heightened awareness you want to be in when a fight starts.

Similarly, when a crisis arises in a company, the leaders must exude "command presence." They must operate in different mental states depending on circumstances. Leaders have their own styles, however, when conditions dictate, they often need to be tough as nails. They know how to select the exact leadership style for the crisis at hand. People desperately want a strong leader who will take command and will get them through the crisis. Think of what Jack Casey did when I called him in Seattle to tell him our new Alaskan operation was drowning in an unanticipated avalanche of packages.

Step 3: Have a Backup Plan

A seasoned guitar player always brings a backup instrument and extra strings to a performance. Tennis players carry extra rackets to a tournament in the event their favorite one breaks. *Isn't this a sign of being a thoroughly prepared professional?*

Your industry might not be music or sports, but you can imagine what a backup plan would look like in your company. This is your go-to strategy when the unexpected strikes.

In the next chapter, you'll see all these principles in practice. We faced a group of employees acting as though they had a boss, one they didn't much like, rather than a leader. They were following a bully, acting far outside the principles that drive UPS. You'll see a group of leaders doggedly educating them out of that mindset. Come with me to choir practice.

How *You* Can Deliver

- Take responsibility for building a culture based on integrity.
- Perform periodic checkups on your team. Address those people who are performing below standards.
- Establish continuous training and development programs.
- Surround yourself with courageous people who are willing to step up and tell you the truth.
- Expect the unexpected. Don't leave anything to chance when planning. Have a backup plan and practice dry runs.

CHAPTER 8

Fostering Positive Interactions

A fter about two years as an operations supervisor working under the wings of upper management, I was promoted to center manager. With the promotion came an assignment to an operation that had more than 100 employees; for the first time in my career, I was truly on my own and had full responsibility for the results we attained.

Although center managers at UPS still have the full support of upper management, as well as numerous other resources available to them, they are completely in charge of and accountable for everything that goes on within their operation. Simply put, the buck stops with them. *They have officially left the nest.* Maybe they fly and maybe they don't.

The particular operation I was put in charge of was both legendary and infamous, but not in a good way. Just about every conceivable human relations problem lived within the walls of that building, and the feeling of *us versus them* was deeply entrenched in the culture. When I learned my first assignment as a center manager would be at this location, I knew immediately I was being thrown into the lion's den.

When I walked in the door that first day, sure enough, the lions were waiting. It was obvious they were hungry for some fresh meat. When I was introduced as the new manager, I was greeted with hissing, booing, and many more one-fingered salutes than I care to mention.

Over the weeks that followed, I spent countless hours with my supervisors trying to understand just what the heck was going on and how this place had gotten into such a dismal state. In response, they proudly showed me the mountains of warning letters, reprimands, and suspensions they had issued.

This reinforced my initial impression that an all-out war was going on between management and our rank-and-file employees. Both sides, it appeared, were fully entrenched in a win-at-all-costs position, and the price our company had already paid was sky high. It was clear to me that management had failed and drastic changes were necessary.

The hostilities had to end and the oversized egos had to be put on hold. As the center's new manager, my reputation was on the line. My job and everything I had worked toward depended on my ability to turn this situation around. Losing was not an option.

Know When to Discard Existing Tactics and Start Fresh

I decided to go against the grain and discarded the existing management's failed tactics. I took aggressive action to set a new course that would mean an entirely different way of doing things from that point on. I felt we needed a fresh start, so I called all the supervisors together for a meeting to lay out my plan.

"We are going to try something new and completely out of the ordinary," I told them, "and you need to get on board—even if it means swallowing your pride. From this point forward, we are going to have zero discipline: that is, no more warning letters, reprimands, suspensions, or any other form of punishment."

You could hear a pin drop.

I insisted there would be no negative verbal or nonverbal communication. This meant that each supervisor and I would make high-frequency, short-interval contacts with every employee every single day. These interactions were to be about something of interest to the employee, maybe even a compliment, and I would not tolerate any sarcastic or disparaging remarks.

"Say anything positive. Anything," I told them, "or just make a passing nonconfrontational remark—like 'Good morning.'"

This meant my supervisors had to know something personal and meaningful about each of their employees to be able to say, "Hey, good job yesterday!" or "How's your family?" or "Did you see the game last night?" For starters, I suggested they talk about news, sports, and weather. They were to talk about job-related issues only if the message was recognizing an employee who had done something well.

Over time, nonconfrontational, positive interactions became routine every time anyone in management had contact with an employee. It took a while, but eventually we broke the ice with a few of them. We were "catching them doing something right"—and saying so. Even the most hard core people appreciate a compliment that is delivered sincerely.

At no time did we compromise policy or sacrifice the company's high standards. We simply worked on being good at building relationships and setting aside the old practice of attacking people. If we could open up a line of communication with just a few of our people, I believed the rest would follow in time.

About a mile from our building was a little tavern where many of our drivers gathered after work. They called it choir practice. We were determined to break down the barriers, so we decided to join the "choir." Although you won't find this method in any UPS supervisor's best-practices handbook, we needed radical new ways of thinking to break down the walls that divided us. So, one night after work, off to choir practice we went. We went again the next night and the night after that.

The first few times we arrived at the tavern, our employees maintained the code of silence, but we did not give up. We went again and again.

Finally, a couple of them began to loosen up a bit. It's amazing what buying a couple of beers and just plain street talk will do. We could easily relate to them because not many years before we had been in their shoes as drivers.

Our employees finally realized we were not their enemy, just hard-working folks like them trying to make a living. They slowly made us a part of the group. When we arrived at that little tavern, they would wave us over and make room for us to sit at their table. Talk about a major breakthrough!

Those choir practices get the credit for tearing down the barriers that separated us from one another. Ending the chronic negative interactions and mingling with employees after hours created open and honest dialogue that was a welcome change to both sides. As I had hoped, it also carried over to the work environment when everyone was on the clock. There were olive branches and beers all around and we all lived happily ever after.

Nope, Not Quite

There were still a few key holdouts in the employee ranks. One tough guy in particular named Rich was not going along with this deal at all. In fact, he became even more vocal and belligerent after our communication breakthrough. Soon he began an all-out effort to get his people back in the fold and reinstitute the old, hostile way of doing things.

Rich was the most negative, antimanagement human being I had ever met in my life. But because he was extremely smart, calculating, and vocal, he had a following among many of his coworkers. He had dedicated his life to making management's life miserable and he was very good at it.

Now for the Rest of the Story

As I'm sure you can imagine, UPS has very strict safety policies. For example, if a driver has three avoidable vehicle accidents within a twelve-month period, he or she is terminated. Rich had accumulated two avoidable accidents and was getting close to having one drop off his record at the end of his rolling twelve-month reporting period that was quickly approaching. More than once, Rich had made it clear to me that he would be home free in a few days and that we could forget about firing him. Then fate stepped in.

Just minutes before Rich's driving record would clear, the one-in-a-million event happened. I was in my office when all of a sudden I heard a loud *cruuuunch*!

I went out to investigate and discovered that Rich had just had his third accident, hitting the overhead door with the top of his package car. Drivers are trained to never open an overhead door partway; it is either all the way down or all the way up. Rich was in a hurry to get off work so he could get to choir practice and start celebrating the removal of one past accident from his record. In his rush, he had failed to raise the overhead door all the way. This was a rookie mistake and he was keenly aware of the consequences.

So there we were, face to face—just Rich and me. We stood there in total silence, surveying the damage. He knew he was done. A few minutes later, he went to the office and filled out an accident report, knowing this was the end. He could probably see his life spiraling rapidly downward into the gloom of unemployment.

Rich walked into my office, sat down, and said, "I guess this is one I'm not going to get out of." Then he started talking about how he would turn in his uniforms. He was resigned to the fact he was going to be terminated.

After inspecting the vehicle and the overhead door, I could see there wasn't any significant damage to the door and just a minor scratch in the paint on the package car. Still, it was an avoidable accident and Rich was not likely to avoid termination. But then I thought, "Should I take the biggest chance of my career? Is this a decision for the take-a-calculated-risk zone?" "Rich," I said, "you've been a pain in my neck, but inside I think you're basically a good guy [all my fingers and toes were crossed]. I am willing to take a chance on you with the hope that you'll take a chance on me. Give me that accident report."

Rich handed me the report. I tore it up and threw it in the wastebasket. "See you in the morning," I said.

Now, UPS takes avoidable accidents seriously and would likely take disciplinary action against a manager who did what I did that day. Nonetheless, I took the calculated risk this once in the hope that it would help me turn around a bad situation.

This tough, hard core guy broke down in tears. Not able to talk, he slowly walked out. For the first time, he did not make choir practice.

Although working relationships were much improved, we still had an absenteeism problem with a few of Rich's loyal followers. We knew the absences were all contrived and the excuses fake, especially the Monday morning ones. We believed many of the hard core employees who continued to refuse to go along with the new deal were conspiring and taking turns calling in sick.

The morning after his run-in with the overhead door, Rich walked into the office a half hour before start time. Without saying a word, he looked at the dispatch report, which showed the names of those who had called in sick. He got on the phone and started calling everyone on the list. Each call was a quick, one-sided conversation.

The whole office could hear him as he made each call. He got right to the point. "This is Rich. I see you called in sick today. Unless you're checking into a hospital, you best get your lazy behind to work right now!"

I could hardly believe what I was hearing. Those people who were too sick to work either experienced a healing miracle, or Rich had suddenly transformed into Florence Nightingale, RN.

Within the hour, every single one of them came to work. Word got around quickly and the long-time absenteeism problem vanished—literally—overnight.

That was just the beginning. As I said, Rich was big, tough, vocal, and intimidating: he could look right through a person

---

HOW LEADERSHIP LOOKS FROM HERE

Leaders Face the Bull

Being a leader isn't easy and some people discover that greater leadership roles simply aren't for them. Eventually, I was going to have to deal with the inevitable conflicts that arise in any organization.

If you have ever seen a bullfight or been to a rodeo, you know it is not smart to mess with the bull. Taking one by the horns seems unthinkable, yet matadors and rodeo clowns learn how to look the big animals in the eye and live to tell about it. When it comes to conflict, every leader needs a little matador and even some rodeo clown in them if they are going to survive.

Everyone under my supervision took their individual and collective cues from me. I had to set the tone and the pace for the work environment. After all, if morale is high and excitement is in the air, it is because someone at the top is thinking and acting right.

Putting others first and helping them reach their dreams, I realized, led to my reaching my own dreams. An old Tibetan proverb bears repeating here: "When he took time to help the man up the mountain, lo, he scaled it himself."

when he talked to them. The employees were scared to death of him. He called a meeting with the employees the following weekend and laid down the law. "Rich did not mince words," said one of the attendees, who later told me about the meeting. "Rich told us that from this point forward, we would all do our jobs, do them well, and all the BS of the past would end here and now!"

The following Monday morning, we saw the radical change we had been hoping for all along. Having Rich in his new role was almost like having another supervisor. He had a huge influence on a good number of the drivers but was now working *with* us, not *against* us.

> **Trust Leads to Loyalty**
>
> I don't think it's any coincidence at all that the most demanding work we do often forges the most meaningful and deepest friendships we have in our lives. Think about it. We all remember the times when things were toughest and who was standing there with us, helping us find our way. Those are things you just don't forget. I know I never have.

I spent much of my career in countries far away from the United States. A big part of my job while working abroad was to teach people new to our company the UPS way of doing business. The more important part of my job, however, was to figure out how to integrate the best of their culture into the best of ours.

This took a lot of time and patience and it taught me how to think differently about people. I gained insights into our sometimes radically different cultures and learned the most effective ways to meld them.

Although the cultures were different, I found that people from Paris to Peru were similar deep inside. People want to be respected and appreciated and have meaningful and positive relationships with their coworkers and the management team. They want to be trusted members of the team. It is up to those in leadership to make it all come together.

Be Secure in Your Role

I learned to welcome both positive and constructive feedback and to encourage healthy debate. Insecure leaders tend to squelch others' opinions and be heavy-handed. In contrast, effective leaders earn their team's trust by being confident, competent, and consistent—not arrogant, disengaged, or hard-headed. When employees see their leader being calm and decisive, day in and day out, that self-assurance exudes a humble confidence. It signals the leader's strong belief in the long-term sustainability of their company. When you pour encouragement into your employees, they experience your vision first-hand and are empowered to play a meaningful part in it. When they trust you at this level, make sure you have their backs and protect them when they make mistakes.

Cultivate Loyalty

Your team has to know that their contributions matter to you. I discovered how to stand up for my people by showing I had faith in them, in good times and especially in bad times. I made it clear that I expected them to do the same. Without two-way loyalty, there can be no trust.

There are no shortcuts to building trust. It takes time. Doing the right thing consistently and taking responsibility when you make mistakes are two of the best ways to start and maintain the trust-building process. Open and honest communication will speed things up, but trust cannot be rushed.

Build a Unified Team

Employees want to bring value to the team and be appreciated for the good things they do. However, after a while, people will not settle for just being noticed; they want to be *known*. Those leaders who go out of their way to know their people and give them a sense of purpose and direction, will earn their loyalty.

Unfortunately, there are obstacles in the way of leaders who want to get to know their people. Too much formality and too little interaction at work prevents people from becoming better known. Cliques often form, which effectively excludes some people and makes it more difficult to build relationships and familiarity.

For the most part, the development of cliques, those "in" and "out" groups in the workplace, is not a good thing. Leaders should make a point of bringing people into their circle instead of excluding them from it. Doing so with intentional focus opens up communication, makes people feel they are part of the team and fosters a cohesive unit.

No one should feel like they are isolated or excluded from the *entire* team. When cliques form, other members of the team who are not in them will form subgroups and thus dilute the cohesiveness. You no longer have one team, but instead multiple teams with members who may not cross boundaries to help members of the "other" team, creating an us-versus-them environment. It's up to leaders to make sure this does not happen.

Do you take breaks or go to lunch on a regular basis with a small select group of people? If so, you are part of the problem. Inclusiveness begins with the leaders' behavior. Including some people in your circle while excluding others reeks of favoritism, sways opinions, and creates suspicion. If you treat the people in your clique differently, others know it and talk about it, at some point, it will hit you right between the eyes. You may think that having your own "in" group of friends within the ranks is okay.

It is not. It violates the *trust rule.*

Some people are more comfortable being around their select group, but a leader thinks about how the rest of the team may feel from the outside looking in. They want to be part of that group and often connect the perception of being excluded with not having value, not being noticed, and not being known. Build teamwork, loyalty, and commitment by creating a cohesive, one-group environment with a collective vision of the future.

Build teamwork, loyalty, and commitment by creating a cohesive, one-group environment with a collective vision of the future.

When Relationships Break Down

Unfortunately, as hard as you may try to build bridges of trust and loyalty, there will be times when relationships break down and conflicts take over. What do you do then?

Speak the Truth and Keep Your Comments Focused

We can build and maintain trust and respect only when we are willing to tell the truth. If you have a problem with a person's performance, say so. Keep your comments focused only on the person's performance and job-relevant behaviors, not their character or emotions. If you disagree with a decision, explain your reasoning and then sincerely attempt to work together to come up with an agreeable solution.

Agree to Disagree

There will be times when you will have to agree to disagree or to ask others to agree to disagree. Common ground is not always available and sometimes people are not willing to budge. As a leader, you are the negotiator, the peacemaker, and the mediator. You are also the ultimate decision maker.

Keep your emotions out of it and focus on what is best for your people and your organization. Listen to all sides of it and deal with the facts. Ask questions, then challenge those refusing to see any position but their own. Try to show each of the disagreeing parties why they need to reevaluate their positions and why they are not yet convincing to the other side.

Where the issues are complex, you may have to buy some time to get others involved. It may take further research and discussions. If compromise is not the right solution, tactfully explain why your decision to end the dispute was made. Try not to step on egos, but realize that making unpopular decisions is just part of being the leader.

Move On

Mature people are normally able to reach the other side of a conflict and still respect one another. When all parties maintain respect despite their differences, relationships grow stronger and the team matures. The key to reinforcing the bonds of trust is to see those with diverse opinions as allies, not opponents. After all, you are on the same team, working toward the same goals. Let opposing views help you make better decisions. View the goal of conflict resolution not as victory, but unity.

> *View the goal of conflict resolution not victory, but unity.*

What's behind you is in the past and not in your future, so when a tough decision has to be made, make it. Allow all team members to have their say, weigh the facts, make the best decision you can, and then move on.

How *You* Can Deliver

- Meet hostility and resistance with genuine and sincere engagement, and with concern and respect for the other person.
- When your people fall short, respond immediately with your support.
- Avoid subgroups. Create joint projects that pull everyone together. Promote the concept of one unified team.
- When relationships break down, shoot straight, speak the truth, and agree to disagree when appropriate.
- When necessary, make the tough decisions and move on.

CHAPTER 9

Moving Forward

Overcome Inertia

Many folks resist change; yet without change, progress is minimal or nonexistent. Truthfully, it is much easier to play it safe and stay comfortable, at least for a little while. Playing it safe all the time is what weak leaders do.

When the downward pull of complacency sets in, fear of change often robs us of the courage needed to lead effectively.

If you want to keep climbing the leadership mountain, you must overcome inertia. As you do this, you will develop a habitual bias for initiating action that keeps things moving until change is embraced. The fact is, sooner or later, you won't have a choice.

The challenge is to determine which changes need to be made and when. Change, for the sake of change, can be beneficial at times, but be careful that you're not just moving the trash around into new piles to make the room look better.

If you want to accomplish something great, then *do something*. If you want to be mediocre, take the path of least resistance and keep on doing what's always been done. There are very few things as powerful as initiative; combined with persistence, you're bound to go farther faster.

How to Overcome Inertia
1. Describe the goal and why it's important to the team and the company.
2. Ensure that the reward for acting exceeds the effort.
3. Describe the negative consequences for failure to act.
4. List all the tasks necessary to deliver the results.
5. Provide adequate resources.
6. Ensure skills are adequate.
7. Make a plan and a schedule.
8. Find someone to cheer you on.
9. Take your first step forward.

Be Open to New Technology

When I was district manager in Oregon, we took bold steps to enhance service to our customers through a new, state-of-the-art technology. It was called the Delivery Information Acquisition Device (DIAD)—the handheld electronic unit that scans packages delivered by UPS drivers.

We tested it first at one of our package operations near Portland, as the manufacturer was nearby. The new technology was a real boon for us; it revolutionized the delivery business and changed the information flow on packages forever. The DIAD greatly enhanced service and at the same time made the driver's job much more efficient and considerably easier.

With the introduction of the DIAD, the old, slow way of manually writing information on paper forms should have quickly faded into history. But, as with many instances when a new technology invades an industry, the quick fade into history didn't happen.

You'd naturally think the DIAD would have been welcomed by all with open arms, but it was a radical departure from how our drivers had been doing their jobs for many years. That old clipboard was what they knew; as we know, change does not come easy.

The majority of drivers who converted to the DIAD raved about how much easier it made their job and how much their customers liked the device. However, there was still a small group of drivers who weren't fully on board with the plan and the pushback began in full force. I met with the group to ask them to give the DIAD a chance, but they told me, in no uncertain terms, the death of the DIAD was imminent. Subgroups were beginning to form within the ranks.

After a few months, however, it was obvious the vast majority of drivers were very happy with the new system, so I decided to hold a meeting with all the drivers. I announced that the test was complete and it was not an option; *everyone* had to use the DIAD or everyone had to go back to manual recording on paper.

We darned near had a riot and many of the drivers became very vocal. One driver yelled out, "Who wants to keep the DIAD?" Hands instantly went up and the vote was 100 percent for keeping the DIAD and zero against. Even the last few holdouts joined with their fellow drivers and voted in favor of it once they saw which direction things were headed. Peer pressure is an amazing thing to watch.

Without leadership and willingness to go up against inertia, that team of drivers could have resisted the DIAD much longer— but it would have been to the detriment of both the individual drivers and the company as a whole. I couldn't let that happen.

Aim for Success, Not to Impress

UPS is a worldwide powerhouse, yet we still believe in a no-frills management style and a culture that entrusts and empowers all of its employees to carry out the mission. It's a big ship but one that remains nimble—always learning, always listening, and always improving.

People who are not pretentious, nor all that interested in impressing others, navigate the ship. It is this organizational humility that runs through the veins of UPS employees and keeps them striving to become better.

What makes UPS so efficient?

The dedicated people who have an unrelenting commitment to success make the UPS family what it is. They are the work-horses who never lose sight of their purpose, doing whatever it takes to grease the gears that keep the big brown machine's wheels turning. They have honed the delivery business from a science into a fine art.

Because highly effective leaders understand the difference between success and failure, efficiency often comes down to the basics, the simple little things that are often overlooked in less successful companies. These types of leaders don't waste time trying to impress anyone. They are workhorses—not *show horses.* They go about their business and focus on getting the job done. Doing their work provides them with satisfaction and inspires them to grow stronger as leaders and that's all they really need. If they are noticed, fine—but they are not driven by the desire to wear a crown and be in the spotlight. In fact, the best leaders I know shy away from it.

I wish we had more leaders like this in business today. So much more would be accomplished and so many more team members could share in the achievements.

When there's cause for celebration, notice how the show horses are the first to step into the spotlight. Yet, when there's trouble, they head to the barn. You will go a lot farther, with longer-lasting results, if you follow the workhorse's lead.

Workhorse leaders have a whatever-it-takes attitude and will knock down walls to complete the mission. Unlike the show horses, they are eager to get into the thick of things and take advantage of times when they can roll up their sleeves and go to work. In the end, people following this kind of leader are happier and more productive; they will be loyal to the workhorse and, eventually, put the show horse out to pasture.

A Whale of a Story

We learned again the value of fielding a team of workhorses rather than individual stars on a project of unprecedented scope. Into the storm we went and the UPS culture is, I believe, the reason the assignment turned out as it did.

A call came in with a request for us to ship a rather large package. We carefully chose a UPS team for the task and they immediately went to work.

The oversized package we were hired to transport was Keiko, the 7,700-pound killer whale that starred in the movie *Free Willy*. Our job was to move him from Mexico City to his new home at an aquarium in Newport, Oregon.

Our UPS team and loadmasters met, extensively, with the aquarium's staff to come up with a plan.

First, UPS had to reengineer a C-130 air freighter. The interior of the aircraft would have to be retrofitted to secure the custom holding tank that would contain Keiko. We would need to install a marine life-support system and an onboard laboratory. These resources enabled aquarium veterinarians to proactively monitor the status of Keiko by continuously checking his vital signs during the trip.

Getting Keiko on the plane was no easy task. The journey began with picking up the four-ton whale, believed to be sixteen to seventeen years old, at the Reino Aventura amusement park in Mexico City. Keiko was hoisted into our huge, water-filled tank and then transported by truck to the Mexico City airport. The route to the airport was lined with thousands of people waving goodbye to the killer whale who had won over many fans during his ten years at the amusement park.

Once aboard the aircraft, the team set environmental controls to ensure Keiko's comfort during the nine-hour flight, with fuel stops in Monterrey, Mexico, and Phoenix, Arizona. The plane required long takeoffs and landings and gradual turns while in the air to avoid unnecessary discomfort to the killer whale.

People traveled hundreds of miles to welcome Keiko and cheering crowds gathered when the plane landed safely. Then we moved Keiko from the Newport Airport to the Oregon Coast Aquarium. It became a national news event as each stage of the giant celebrity's trip to his new home in the United States was made safely—thanks to the UPS team.

This unusual job required a specialized team composed of many people with different skills and talents working together with precision and care to deliver Keiko. Whether it's a small envelope or a large package that fills an entire airplane, there is always a clearly defined method for doing the job right.

Develop Self-Assessment Skills

Sometimes leaders forget that their primary job is to get things done through others. You have to be quick to recognize weaknesses in the team and step in before they become problems. This means taking time to recognize your *own* plusses and minuses.

We all have to accept that we have limitations. This has nothing to do with our overall intelligence or experience. It has everything to do with knowing when to fill the gaps with people who are strong where we are weak.

Self-assessment is a critical skill that requires continual development throughout your career. Your ability to admit your weaknesses is a sign of great wisdom and personal strength. It doesn't make you ineffective, just honest. People who admit they don't

> **HOW LEADERSHIP LOOKS FROM HERE**
>
> ### Leaders Find Solutions
>
> Even though we hadn't shipped a whale before, we knew there was a right way to do it. There always is. The right way leads to the optimal outcome for everyone involved, including a four-ton mammal.
>
> UPS is relentless when it comes to establishing proper methods to do almost any job and each step in the process exists for a reason. Whether it's how to properly back up a package car, walk on slippery ice, or even how to move a huge whale through customs, chances are there's a method to address it.
>
> The methods, fine-tuned for more than 100 years, have become a science that allows people to do their jobs in the safest way possible with the least amount of effort. By following the proper procedures, maximum efficiency can be reached.

know everything project a confidence that their coworkers value. People who can't are always found out—usually sooner rather than later—and their influence is greatly diminished.

Since everyone realizes that it's impossible to know everything, you'd think it would be relatively easy to make that admission. Believe me, it is not! Show horse leaders are fixated on appearances and they find it extremely difficult to admit their shortcomings.

When you are candid with your team members, you may be surprised by how much easier it becomes to stay more focused and get more accomplished. In order to stay grounded, though, you may want to do a periodic self-assessment checkup. Here's how.

Be You

You can't be someone else. Don't try to be.

Be Present

Give people your full and undivided attention. When you are with someone, don't let anything distract you. Those phone calls and messages can wait until later.

When you allow distractions to interrupt conversations with others, not only are you being rude, you're sending a message that other things are more important than the people who are with you. They came to talk with you, not to watch you act as though you are too busy.

Shut out the rest of the world. It will still be there when you return. As I've said before, communication is good, but connective communication is better.

Be Humble

Don't try to know it all. Don't act like you know it all. Don't try to do it all. Don't pretend you know how to do something better than someone else. Arrogance is a culture killer.

When people in your group are better than you at a particular task (and, more often than not, they *should* be), recognize it and delegate to capitalize on their strengths. In other words, let them do what they do best and you do what you do best.

Approach Each Day as Your Last as a Leader

The daily grind gets a bad rap. Few people would say they wake up excited about the grind—that's because it's human nature to take the path of least resistance. *But what if this mindset changed for you?*

What if, instead, each day you approached the grind as a workhorse leader? If each day you arrived at work fully attuned to your unique opportunity to improve your team's ability to succeed? If providing the highest levels of service became your primary focus at the beginning of every day?

Without a grinder, there is no coffee. Roll up your sleeves and get your hands dirty. White shirts and ties are frequently overrated.

Leading from the front and getting involved (without getting in the way) usually brings positive results. When you let your people know you are with them on the playing field and that you will work longer and harder than anyone else, they will increase their efforts, too. Preaching from your comfortable office is one thing; walking the walk on the front line with your people is something entirely different. You can pretend to care but you can't pretend to be there.

> *Let your people know you are with them on the playing field and that you will work longer and harder than anyone else.*

From experience, you will sense when to jump into the grind and when to stay out of the way. NFL teams devote enormous resources to studying films, reviewing game scenarios, and learning from the careful analysis of both their wins *and* their losses.

Teams in the business world should be no different. Study both your successes and failures and make adjustments as necessary. One framework for doing this is what I call the good, the bad, and the ugly review.

Study Your Successes and Failures and Make Adjustments

The Good

What's working? There will be some places where your team is firing on all cylinders. Build up these areas for sustained success and pour more resources into them so they become the fortification of your operation. The *good* part of the review will also highlight accomplishments you can celebrate as a team, allowing you an ongoing opportunity to praise members for positive results.

The Bad

What's not working? Maybe deadlines were pushed back, commitments missed, and sometimes customers lost. When the *bad* is clearly identified, your team has the opportunity to regroup and refocus—make this a time for a "lessons learned" session.

The Ugly

What got ugly? Most of the time, regular team reviews will reveal that things are either good or bad. But occasionally, you and your team will uncover something that is just plain *ugly*—worse than bad.

It could be gross misconduct, negligence, sabotage, or deliberate indifference resulting in a defective product or service. Regardless of what it is, it will likely result in significant damage to the reputation of your company. When faced with an *ugly*, you need to take action immediately. Make specific assignments to fix an *ugly* in a no-holds-barred approach. Say it like it is.

A little fear in the air may be necessary to set things right. If the *ugly* happens to be a slacking manager, you may have to have a serious career discussion. Management personnel, or anyone for that matter, found lying down on the job or doing the minimum required is contagious; it is a bad disease that spreads fast, so it must be isolated and stopped.

The realities of doing business in a team-oriented culture dictate there are times when talk and second chances just don't work. Sometimes, you have to lay down the law and face the *ugly* immediately.

I Didn't Know Jack

As a young, newly promoted division manager for UPS in Seattle, I was anxious to make a good impression at my first staff meeting. As fate would have it, this was also the first meeting for our new district manager, a man named Jack.

Jack was a rugged, rather large Irishman who grew up in a tough neighborhood in New York City. As you might expect, Jack's reputation preceded him. He was known as a fearless street fighter who pulled no punches and he carried this rough-and-tumble attitude with him into the office. When people didn't meet his expectations, he wasn't shy about letting them know it.

On the other hand, Jack was also known to have an incredibly big heart and wouldn't think twice about going out of his way to take care of his people. He made the work fun and interesting and was always in on the action—working side by side with his team and personally helping them through their most difficult times. You always knew where you stood with Jack.

Back to the monthly staff meeting: It was structured with a set agenda that was sent out well in advance of the meeting— attendees had weeks to prepare for it. Nothing about that had changed with the arrival of our new district manager, so everyone knew what to expect. Even I, the newest manager in the room, was as well prepared as I could possibly be.

At 8:00 a.m. sharp, Jack walked in and called the meeting to order. All the chatter in the room came to an abrupt halt. Each of us mentally prepared to present our reports to the new man in charge.

After a few introductory comments, Jack called on the first manager to report. Visibly nervous, he explained he had just flown in that morning and had not had time to prepare for the meeting.

Big mistake!

Jack lowered his glasses and with a face that took on a brighter shade of red with each passing second, he glared at the manager for what seemed to me like forever. I'm certain that the tempera-ture in the room rose to about 1,000 degrees Fahrenheit—I know that each of us could hear our hearts pounding in our chests as we imagined the terrible consequences our unprepared colleague was about to suffer.

Sure enough, the Irishman from New York asked in a loud, angry voice, "Do you not have a staff? Did you forget how to delegate?!"

And that was just the beginning. The verbal beating went on and on with no end in sight. I felt sure we were going to witness a homicide before it was all over.

I began to wonder if Jack would notice if I didn't come back after the break. In fact, I was seriously thinking of ways I could get demoted in a hurry to my familiar old job. It may not have paid as much, but I was pretty sure I wouldn't end up with any black eyes either.

Finally, the pummeling stopped and Jack sat back in his chair and casually announced, "No problem . . . the rest of us will sit here and wait while you step out and put your reports together."

And that's exactly what we did. We sat quietly in that conference room—in dead silence—for nearly five long hours. No breaks, no lunch, no talk. Jack didn't move, nor did we. We didn't dare. The silence was finally broken when the manager reentered the room and gave his report. The meeting ended a little after midnight.

Maybe the lesson Jack taught us during the course of our prolonged first encounter with him was overkill, but we sure knew who was in charge. Jack was nobody to play games with. He was as demanding as any manager could possibly be.

Anyway, after that first staff meeting the word got around fast and you can rest assured no one ever showed up unprepared again for anything that had to do with Jack. I know I sure didn't. Although my own management style differed greatly from Jack's, his way of drawing a clear line in the sand from the very beginning was effective. He drove a stake in the ground and left no doubt in anyone's mind that there was a new sheriff and "The Bad and The Ugly" weren't welcome in his town—only "The Good."

Balance Results and the "Big Picture"

It's so tempting to think that only the numbers matter and every-thing else is secondary. Don't fall into this trap. Results are important, but they are not the *only* things that matter. If, for example, your production record is the only metric you've got for measuring the health of your organization, you may be missing what really matters: the quality of your service. It is important to measure all relevant factors.

Keep your sights on the big picture—production and quality should go hand in hand. It's a balancing act, for sure. Lose pro-duction and you lose profits. Lose your quality and you lose your business.

My friend Jimmy Collins, former president and COO of Chick-fil-A, once told me about a time he visited a well-known competitor's fast-food hamburger joint. He placed an order for a bag of french fries and then he waited—and waited. While he waited, he noticed the employees rushing order after order of fries to the drive-thru window, while completely ignoring him. He finally lost his patience and demanded to talk with the manager.

Jimmy asked the manager why he hadn't yet received his or-der of french fries, although her staff kept rushing orders of them right past him to the drive-thru window. The manager re-plied that the corporate office was timing the staff on how quickly they filled drive-thru orders, so that was their top prior-ity. Jimmy then calmly asked, "Do they measure how quickly you serve customers *inside* the restaurant?"

This is a classic example of missing the mark. Their intentions were good, but they got it only half right. Measuring the deliv-ery time at the drive-thru window was a "right" thing, just not the *only* right thing. When you fail to measure *all* the right things, you get the wrong results.

How *You* Can Deliver

- Take charge. Do what is right; when conditions dictate it, be as tough as you have to be.
- Keep teams engaged with a sense of purpose. Give genuine and specific praise when earned and do it often.
- Develop and continuously practice the skill of self-assessment.
- Measure the relevant things that drive your business.
- Keep everyone focused on the most important thing: your customer.

CHAPTER 10

Prepare for Places Unexpected

I was extremely grateful and proud to be a UPS delivery driver from a small town in northern Idaho. I never even considered the possibility that I might someday end up traveling the world as president of UPS International; that thought was beyond my wildest dreams.

My path through the organization spanned close to four decades and I served in many different positions within the company over my career. However, the most unexpected one of them all began with a conversation one afternoon in the office of our then CEO, Jim Kelly. I will forever remember Jim's words as he officially promoted me to president of UPS International.

Jim said to me:

> Ron, you operate a little differently than most, maybe even a little radically; but you have done pretty well and understand the international business. In your new assignment, you will have the authority and freedom to operate and do whatever is necessary to make our operations outside of the United States successful, within policy, of course.

I was grateful to be given so much freedom to do it my way, or that's at least what I *thought* I heard. Maybe I interpreted it as what I wanted to hear. Regardless, it was a dream come true for me; I felt like an angel who had finally earned his wings.

The international part of our business was not doing well. It had expanded quickly and was going through some serious growing pains. To obtain operating rights and expand our services, we became partners with some companies that, to that point, did not operate up to UPS standards.

Many people were working hard, but our international business continued to flounder. I felt we needed a new look and some radical changes. The current way we were operating just wasn't getting it done and over the years there seemed to be little progress.

My management team and I immediately went to work, focusing on opening some long-locked doors and turning the place upside down. Within a year, it landed right-side up. It's incredible what happens when you give your managers free rein and provide them with the resources they need.

Two things happened very quickly: first, we rightsized the workforce; second, we empowered our management team to run their businesses as they saw fit. It could not have worked any other way.

Never Micromanage

As difficult as it is to let go, higher-level managers must trust their people to get the job done while staying out of their way. I never hesitated to put boundaries in place and stay close to the action. But, at the same time, I gave my managers the freedom to operate as they saw fit and to do whatever they believed was necessary.

These are the same freedoms Jim Kelly gave me. Yes, mistakes were made. In fact, I made a lot of them. But when my management team wisely used those freedoms to do it their way, the little mistakes were more than compensated for by the big things that brought about positive results.

In a big world tasked with leading a huge operation, micromanaging was out of the question and time was not on our side. We were given the latitude to make critical decisions and the freedom to operate as we saw fit. At the same time, our international team had strong support from Jim and the corporate staff. Eventually, it all came together; in just over a year, International became profitable for the first time.

Set Boundaries

Allowing people the freedom to operate using their own style is important, but it must be within the framework of the organization's culture and policies. Leaders are environment shapers—they set boundaries for their people and foster productivity within appropriate, well-defined borders. They are respected and followed because they do the right things, the right ways, at the right times. They trust their people and *Foster productivity within appropriate, well-defined borders.* give them the authority necessary to get things done and lead in their own way. This starts with the way they communicate with the members of their team.

Never was this principle more clear to me than one afternoon when I was in my office in Germany, trying to review and approve a time-sensitive proposal for an important customer. My absolute deadline was 5:00 p.m., as the customer was scheduled to meet with me to review our offering at that time.

It was already after 4:00 p.m. and I was working diligently to read the thick proposal. Suddenly, my administrative assistant, Kelly, entered my office with a pressing problem that couldn't wait. When I turned my attention to focus on her issues, I suddenly realized I had forgotten to submit a travel voucher request for an upcoming trip.

For a moment, I stopped listening to Kelly while I jotted down a reminder to myself about the travel voucher. The phone rang and, of course, I just had to answer it.

Frustrated, Kelly walked out of my office just as I asked her to please hold on while I answered a call. A few moments later, she was back at my office door to announce that my 5 o'clock appointment was coming down the hall to sign the proposal.

Sound familiar?

With all that was going on in those few moments, I slipped into *distraction distortion mode* by failing to listen to Kelly's concerns and meet my deadline—two failures at one time. Both of the things that I lost sight of were far more important than anything I allowed to distract me that afternoon. I failed to set boundaries for *myself.*

Communicate Effectively

The primary goal in any communication is *connection.* You must connect clearly so people get the message you are trying to convey.

> *Connect clearly so people get the message you are trying to convey.*

They have to feel your passion if you want their own enthusiasm and dedication for the cause to increase.

Listen Closely

The most effective way to connect is to show that you understand not just the words another person speaks, but also the meaning and intent behind their words. To do this consistently, you have to listen closely to comprehend the message that's truly being sent. If you only pretend to listen without paying attention to cues like facial expressions and body language, you may miss the message entirely.

Asking questions and requesting clarification demonstrate that you are interested and that you are *really listening* to what is being said, not just *hearing*. A simple, yet effective practice is to have no barriers (e.g., sit on the same side of the table), find things you have in common, and maintain eye contact with the person who is speaking with you. This habit helps you focus on the words as well as the actual message the other person is trying to convey. Your ears will tend to follow your eyes and this combination will make it harder for your mind to drift and miss the nonverbal signals the speaker may be sending. People who talk about the great communicators they have met always say one thing: "She [or he] made me feel as though I was the only person in the room."

Say what you mean—when your words are scarce, the ones you do say become all the more important. What you say carries a lot of weight. When there's nothing more to say, don't say it.

Filter What You Say

Ten days after retiring from UPS, I started attending classes in a police academy and have been a law-enforcement officer ever since. Police officers have a simple rule for themselves when dealing with a particularly obnoxious person: *If it feels good, don't say it.* The next time you are about to say something that could be insensitive or detrimental, take a minute to first put your thoughts through this filter:

- Is it true?
- Is it necessary and is it necessary to say it *now*?
- Is it respectful, or is there a respectful way I can say it?

Everyone knows what happens whenever you forget to put the filter in your coffeemaker; you start your day with a mess. If you forget to filter your words as a leader, confusion reigns, feelings are hurt, emotions spew out, and often what was intended to be helpful turns out to be degrading. When you take the time to run your words through the filter, you might be surprised at what you decide to keep to yourself.

Consider the Weight of Your Words

Because your team listens to everything you say and they sometimes rehash those words endlessly, looking for any hidden meaning that might be directed at them personally, choose your words wisely. Right or

Choose your words wisely.

wrong, fair or unfair, this is just the way it is when you are the person in charge. In fact, you should be aware of those who are looking for reasons to find something adverse in your comments. They are out there.

The Heat of the Moment in Hawaii

There were times when I found myself talking when I should have been listening. On one occasion, I found myself in some very hot water while on a special assignment in Hawaii heading up a small team of UPSers. The goal was to integrate the UPS culture and operating methods into a well-established, local delivery company that UPS had acquired.

The acquisition gave us instant access to an established operation on the island and a great opportunity to build our brand locally. It was, basically, a good company. However, it came with a culture much different from that of UPS. The business was family-owned and the owners had considerable trouble holding a few problem people accountable. They tolerated bad behavior from employees who had been with them for many years. One individual in particular was poisoning the organization. His name was Lance; along with a negative attitude, he had a severe attendance problem. He was constantly absent on Mondays, averaging three out of four a month.

Lance openly bragged about getting away with this behavior and he actively encouraged his coworkers to do the same. When challenged, his excuse was that hard weekend partying meant he was too tired to work on Mondays. I gave him an A+ in arrogance. He thrived on telling management what he would and wouldn't do, letting them know they could do nothing about it. In a sense, he was right; in the former company, they had let him get away with it for years. I decided not to delegate this one and told Lance, in no uncertain terms, that his world was about to change.

I, personally, talked to him each time he crossed the line, increasing the intensity at every step and documenting the details of our discussions. After one such meeting, I talked with the previous owner, telling him I was out of patience and that I had given Lance his final warning with clear instructions to be at work on Monday.

The owner replied, "That's asking for a lot. Lance is normally sick on Mondays and has been for as long as I can remember." Biting my tongue and sensing no support there, it was obvious I was on my own in dealing with Lance.

Then it all came to a head. On the following Monday, Lance's package car was loaded full of packages, but, of course, there was no Lance.

I asked his new supervisor where Lance was. After reminding me it was Monday, he informed me that Lance had called in sick. I lost it.

I told the supervisor, "If he is sick, he needs to be in a hospital to find out the cause of these Monday health problems. Send an ambulance to his house." And that's exactly what he did.

I realized I had made a major mistake when Hawaii Five-O walked into my office a few hours later and issued me a strong warning, leaving me with a stiff bill for the cost of the ambulance. Frankly, I was lucky I didn't go to jail.

Lance showed up for work the rest of the week, but it didn't last. The following Monday, he called in sick again; when he arrived at work on Tuesday morning, I terminated him. I was a little surprised when the former owners of the company and several of the employees commented it was about time.

Clearly, my order to the supervisor in the heat of the moment to call an ambulance was wrong. I should have kept my temper under control. Thank goodness, he told the police that he had been ordered to do it by me; that's how they ended up in my office giving me a well-deserved lecture. I wish I had known about filters back then and better understood the weight of words. I guess some lessons come harder than others.

Think Your Message through Carefully

Avoid giving people a reason to mistrust you.

Give careful thought to your message so you do not have to go back to explain what you meant to say the first time. Set parameters for yourself through your carefully chosen words.

Avoid giving people a reason to mistrust you.

Remind your team members that effective communication is crucial to connecting with one another and building strong working relationships. Carefully consider what you say, when you say it, how you say it and—most importantly—whether you should say it at all.

If you want your employees to function effectively as a team, get them actively involved so they know what's going on. There should be no secrets, no mysteries, and no surprises. Not doing this will throw the rumor mills into action and you will find yourself devoting far too much time and energy to putting out fires.

When you encourage collaboration, your team feels directly involved in the objectives and they will be committed to achieving them. This does not mean all team members will get their way, but *they do need to have their way considered.* You, alone, are responsible for the final decision, but your best decisions should be based upon a collaborative process and receiving as much relevant information as possible.

Put Yourself Where the Action Is

Part of being prepared for the unexpected is putting yourself where the action is and making unscheduled visits to see how things are going. Walking around and interacting with your people brings amazing results.

As you take the pulse of your personnel and get an up-close view of what they are doing, you develop a tighter bond with them. Your visits to their workplaces say that you care about what they are doing and send a strong message that what they do matters. These are the times when you make it clear you are open to listening to what people have to say.

Our UPS management team had a distinct advantage. They had risen through the ranks and knew the demands of each and every job in the company. By the way, we always knew when the local management team had caught wind that we were coming to visit their facilities. The smell of fresh paint was a dead giveaway.

Many things surface while you are spending quality time with your people. Occasionally, things come up that need attention and sometimes it just seems that it would have been too simple to resolve them before you dropped in. Think about problems such as mechanical breakdowns in a fleet, computers that frequently fail, or any of those other frustrating issues that pop up. *Are the people in charge correcting them or ignoring them? Are they just giving lip service to company policy or helplessly signaling there is nothing they can do about the breakdowns?*

Mechanical problems are not mechanical problems at all—they are *people* problems that managers must solve. Employees need to have all the necessary tools to do their jobs properly and they need those tools to work perfectly every single day. It is up to their management team to make this happen, no matter how many cages they have to rattle and how far up the chain of command they need to go. Great leaders will bend over backwards and do whatever is necessary to make sure those people on the front line get what they need. *The best of the best take servant leadership to heart.*

Some folks think the whiners, complainers, and squeaky wheels should be ignored. I believe the opposite. In my experience, more often than not, the people with the courage to speak up are the ones trying to make conditions better, thus making the company better.

Even if it is a gripe, it means something is not right and needs a manager's attention. *Who better to tell management how things really are than those who do the job every day?* They may just have a great idea that could improve the way things are done. If nothing else, just the fact that you listened to them and gave them a little attention goes a long way. I couldn't begin to count all the inventions, processes, and improvements within the UPS systems that came from our employees. And this all occurred because people were allowed to share their ideas in the UPS culture of *"we."*

Of course, there will be the serial complainers who just want to complain about everything for no legitimate reason. Their concerns need to be addressed, as they are the ones who can affect morale, often by spreading rumors and ignoring the facts. However, those who speak up with legitimate concerns should always be taken seriously.

If a janitor in a UPS facility had a better idea that would help solve a bottleneck on a loading dock, we wanted to hear it. If a driver had a better idea about how to save fuel, we wanted to hear it. If a clerk had a better idea for ridding ourselves of unnecessary and time-wasting reports, we wanted to hear it.

All you have to do is listen and then take action. Your people are handing you a way to make things better on a silver platter. Take it. Leadership can sprout in unexpected places.

Assess Your Company's Evaluation Program

At UPS, we conducted performance reviews, called Quality Performance Reviews, every six months. Eighty percent of the review was based on hard numbers or completed goals and 20 percent on subjective or softer measurements.

When was the last time you reviewed your company's formal evaluation program with a critical perspective? *Does it accomplish what it was designed for, or does it do more harm than good? Are people looking forward to a fair and constructive review, or do they see it as judgment day? Does it align with your goals and the company's mission?*

Over time, people add elements to performance reviews that are not relevant in the big picture, creating confusion and doing more harm than good. Keep in mind, an evaluation is a person's report card and often determines their pay, selection for a desirable assignment, or opportunity for advancement. Each level of management should not hesitate to challenge the company's approach to evaluation. Ask questions and hold the evaluator accountable. Employees will remember their reviews for a long time, especially if they feel as though they were treated unfairly in the process.

Not everything can be measured and not everything should appear as a cold, hard set of numbers listed on a preprinted evaluation form.

Should intangible things that are not on the evaluation form be considered? You be the judge.

Base your appraisal on performance over the total evaluation period and not just what struck you recently, good or bad. Include those intangible things that are relevant as well.

Leaders Recognize That Not All Performance Criteria Are on the Evaluation Form

Not everything can be measured. Allow flexibility and apply some common sense when evaluating people. I remember hearing about the last driver returning to her UPS center one cold wintry night, with temperatures near the freezing point. After checking out, she entered the locker room and discovered a broken pipe that was flooding the whole place. Fortunately, she noticed a mechanic in the parking lot and ran out to catch him as he was getting into his car to leave for the night. She told him about the broken pipe and he immediately ran back into the building and put his coveralls on. He and the driver worked together for the next four hours fixing the water leak and cleaning up the mess.

Repairing those water pipes was not in their job descriptions, but these two employees took it upon themselves to do what needed to be done that night. They only mentioned it to one other mechanic several months later, who then told me about it.

I mentioned the water incident at evaluation time to each of their managers, who had not heard about this heroic action by their employees either. I told them that while it was certainly up to them, they might want to give the driver and mechanic a nudge to the positive side of their performance evaluations. I went further and recognized them both as Employees of the Year.

Did I mention the night they stayed until the wee hours of the morning fixing the leaky pipe was Christmas Eve?

Job evaluations should be an open, two-way conversation so employees understand their strengths and weaknesses. If there are serious areas of concern, start by asking for their side of the story and focus only on their behavior and the consequences, rather than implying there's a flaw in their character.

The elements on the appraisal form should be based directly on the duties and outcomes in an employee's job description. When an evaluation is based upon the measurable and relevant results, then the person being evaluated will have a clear understanding of what is expected of them and how they are judged. They should never be caught off guard. Put the rules of the game on the table with full transparency for all to see.

How *You* Can Deliver

- Communicate to connect with others. Talk. Listen. Act.
- Carefully consider your words before you say anything that could be hurtful or damaging. Remember to filter your comments.
- Never give others a reason to mistrust you.
- Make walking around a regular part of your management routine.
- Let employees know immediately if you are dissatisfied with their performance, not during a performance review months later.

CHAPTER 11

Signed, Sealed, and Delivered

"The greatest leader is not necessarily the one who does the greatest things. He is the one that gets the people to do the greatest things."—*Ronald Reagan*

Just a few weeks before my retirement, I had the opportunity to observe the night sort at our UPS airport (formerly Clark Air Force Base) in the Philippines. It was one of the top-performing air operations in the world.

During the course of my tour, our division manager Ed introduced me to hundreds of people. Amazingly, he knew the names of every single employee. Even more impressive were the great attitudes of each one of them and the positive comments they made about the company and about Ed.

Although difficult to describe, it was almost a party atmosphere at the airport that night as hundreds of workers unloaded and loaded packages into air containers, while others on the ramp staged the aircraft. They were all working extremely hard, yet they were having fun.

Clearly, there was something special going on and I quickly figured out the source. It was Ed.

I just had to know his secret, so I asked Ed to tell me what made him and his team so darned good. He told me something that night that I will never forget.

With all the modesty in the world and a slight smile, Ed told me the following: "It is my four faiths. I believe in God. I believe in my company. I believe in myself. And I believe in my friends, who just happen to be my employees." Obviously, there is a lot to learn about leading others, but then again maybe all you need is a little faith.

Leaders like Ed have that extra something that makes them special. They figure out how to build teams that are so capable they hit their targets even when the leader isn't around. Their loyalty to one another is unquestioned.

These teams have laser-like focus and endless energy. In a stormy situation, they make the prevailing winds work in their favor. An inspired team can outwork and outwit the competition any day of the week. Ed's team is just one example of what brings success to UPS. The fact is UPS has a whole lot of Eds leading our teams all over the world.

As the policy book said, customers are the reason for UPS's existence and the company remembers that it was created to provide a service. People, reputation, growth, and service remain the core of UPS's success. Although they are not complex, these values have strong meaning and have managed to sustain the company since 1907. Let's summarize a few of the key principles that have contributed to the success of UPS:

- *Provide Opportunities for Ownership.* In 1927, when the company was incorporated as United Parcel Service, both management and nonmanagement personnel were given the opportunity to buy UPS stock. Although several changes have been made to the program since then, this may be the single most important part of the company's culture. It contributes to the high employee retention and gives employees a feeling that UPS is "my company."
- *Promote from Within.* Managers who start with an organization and rise through its ranks are likely to be more aligned, committed, and experienced than those

brought in laterally from the outside. We didn't hire just for a job, but for a career. This has been the company policy from the beginning and every CEO has come up through the ranks. Therefore, we know that anytime we hire a new employee, they could be a future CEO.

- *Be Constructively Dissatisfied.* No matter how successful a company is, leaders should never be satisfied. Once we do something well, we continue to look for ways to do it better. Great companies adapt to changing conditions. They don't deny that perplexing conditions exist, nor do they pretend that markets will remain certain or be kind to them. In fact, they embrace those realities and plan for the certainty of coming storms by staying nimble and agile. They are constructively dissatisfied. Leaders make conditions; they don't become victims of them.
- *Build on the Past While Charting the Future.* We use our corporate values to describe what is important to our organization. We tie in stories, images, and lessons from the company's history to illustrate the fundamentals that are embedded in the UPS culture. Together, these factual accounts allow us to perpetuate a winning mindset that lets us move forward as a unified company.
- *Reward Performance.* The culture at UPS is one of impartiality: each person is on par with all others. Employees advance when they demonstrate more capability than others, show individual merit and performance, and have superior relations and respect for their customers and their peers. This mantra directly ties into our policy of promoting from within.
- *Decentralize Management to Encourage a "Culture of We."* Since the beginning, UPS effectively implemented a

decentralized management philosophy. From the drivers to the most senior executives in the company, we depend on people fulfilling their duties with minimum interference, allowing people to supervise themselves without someone looking over their shoulders. This trust fosters an entrepreneurial spirit of doing their jobs for "their company."

- *Encourage Adaptability.* Adaptability does not require changing in response to every fad or passing trend, but a willingness and preparedness to do so, radically and completely, when it is necessary. This spirit of teamwork and the desire to get behind changes of tremendous operational and organizational value are essential to tackle significant challenges in the environment.

- *Rotate to Develop.* When you rotate people through various positions in a company, they develop and adapt to all aspects of the business, including different localities and cultures, allowing for a deeper understanding of the entire company. You create armies of generalists who develop into specialists later in their careers. This allows managers to understand and appreciate what other people do and how each job vitally contributes to the overall success of the company. The necessity for teamwork becomes obvious when you know how all the roles are integrated.

- *Put the Customer First.* "Anybody can deliver packages, from the small boy in the neighborhood on up to the most extensive delivery systems in the land. The one thing we have to offer that others will not always have is quality."[11] This statement holds true today, just as it has for more than one hundred years.

- *Be Humble.* Most UPSers came from humble beginnings, just as the company started modestly with an investment of $100 and a small office in a basement in Seattle, Washington. This humility drove the company over the years to be a quiet, but unified company— ordinary people with a respect for the company uniting to do extraordinary things. This simple idea fosters teamwork and creates a competitive advantage.

All leadership begins with relationships and the level of trust that exists in them. People have wasted immense amounts of time through the ages arguing whether leaders are born or made. The fact is, it doesn't matter. If you think about it, leaders must have or develop the ability to influence others in some way to achieve their goals. Ministers are looked up to because of their ability to communicate and relate to people. Coaches must motivate their players to give their all. Supervisors in small offices must get their workers to be at their best. The CEO of a multinational billion-dollar company must know how to encourage employees in distant locations to work seamlessly and remain committed to attaining the organization's goals. They all must be trusted and trust their people to deliver.

Napoleon reportedly once said, "Men will work for money, but they'll die for a medal." Great leaders have mastered the ability to inspire followers to walk through fire for them. The secret? Relationships. In good times and bad, they are able to communicate to their team, "We're in this together." A team that truly believes this will be willing to give their all for you, just as Napoleon's followers did for him.

It is obvious there are many things that can produce the kind of leader people are eager to follow. Maybe it's realizing there is more power in "we" than "me." Maybe it's being willing to leave your office and get out on the front line with your people.

The kind of leader you will be is up to you. I hope that the time-tested principles in *Leadership Lessons from a UPS Driver* will keep you thinking—and acting—like a great leader. You have been summoned to lead. There is greatness in you waiting to be unleashed. Now, it's time for you to deliver.

One of our best UPS drivers once told me: "When I arrive at work, I own my job and every part of it. That includes making sure I, personally, don't cause issues for the people who pay me. In fact, I do everything I can in my little world to make them and our company look good." Great leaders do exactly the same thing and then take it a step further: *they do everything they can to make their people and company not only look good, but be good.* Here are a few final points that I believe separate the merely good leaders from the great ones:

- *Understand you are in the people business. People* produce great products and services. If you don't show genuine appreciation to them, you'll only be a marginal leader at best . . . and likely not any kind of leader for long. Never allow yourself to feel entitled by your position or flex your power over followers. Remain humble at all times, even when times are challenging, and especially when things are going great.
- *Be a Servant Leader.* You are to take care of and serve your followers by providing them direction, guidance, encouragement, feedback, counseling, and resources. You are their servant, not the other way around.
- *Be generous.* Be quick to offer a word of encouragement or appreciation and be generous with your resources. It is okay to make a profit. It is not okay to be ruled by greed. Celebrate and give back to your employees in a spirit of abundance.
- *See what you do as more than just a job.* Be passionate about your job, your company, and your people. Leaders don't quit at quitting time, simply because they do not

want to. They are on a roll, in the zone—they have lost track of time. Ideally, you start your day, and after what feels like one hour, look at the clock and see that eight hours have passed.

As the leader, people will look to you to set the pace and keep the team on course. If your team is working late into the night and on weekends on an urgent project, you should be right there with them and not out on the golf course. Your team needs to know you are there to support them in whatever way they need to get the job done.

Certainly, each company is unique and has its own way to deliver its product or service. The lessons in this book have enabled UPS to deliver the best services possible while growing dramatically and still offers financial rewards to employees and shareholders. These lessons in leadership presented here may not always be the best way for you—improvements can always be made and the pursuit to find better ways of doing business never ends.

Regardless, the success of UPS has proved that the company's unique culture works, even on the scale of 435,000 employees. If I could only have a couple of phrases to sum up what makes UPS a great company, I would tell others it all boils down to this: *Determined people working together in a values-based culture that constantly strives to be the best. We, not me.*

Oh, and its heroes wear brown socks.

A Study Guide for Leaders and Their Teams

Y ou can go through *Leadership Lessons from a UPS Driver* in a group setting to help you with team building and leadership training. Using the questions here as a guide, you and your team can develop ways to get better at what you do—individually and together.

Chapter 1: Delivering a Culture

1. What is a values-based culture?
2. How do you align each of the following areas with your organization's values?
   a. PEOPLE (do they know their jobs, the team's goals?)
   b. PRIDE in your organization
   c. APPEARANCE of your people, buildings, and equipment
   d. PROMOTION (do they know what it takes to be considered for increased levels of responsibility?)
   e. PROCESS IMPROVEMENT
   f. COMMUNICATION (how do employees learn of company news?)
   g. COMPANY OWNERSHIP
   h. MENTORING
   i. EMPLOYEE SELECTION
3. What is constructive dissatisfaction?

4. How do your employees, including executive management, show respect and appreciation for each other?
5. How do you welcome new employees to the organization and your team in particular?
6. What exactly do you know about each member of your team?

Chapter 2: Building a Successful Team

1. The question "Do I play my five best or my 'best five'?" is a question every leader faces.
   a. Who are your "best five"?
   b. Who are your five best?
   c. How do you decide which five to play?
   d. Who has the potential to be in the "best five"?
2. What answer would you expect from your team if you asked them, "What is the reason for our success?"
3. Who is your mentor?
4. Who are you mentoring?
5. How are you preparing your team to take maximum advantage of opportunities?
6. Would those under your supervision define you as a boss or a leader? If the former, what do you need to change about your approach to leading?
7. Do you think the quality of an organization is tied more to its leadership or its workforce? Explain your answer.

Chapter 3: Divine Intervention

1. Who on your team seems to always find work that needs to be done, well beyond their assigned duties?
   a. How do you reward or recognize those people?
   b. How can you instill that drive in other team members?

2. Do you know the following about all your team members: their family, where they grew up, hobbies, goals, aspirations, concerns, and anything else that is important in their lives?
3. What do you do to create a sense of fellowship among your employees?
   a. Have you shared the company's history with them?
   b. Have you told them about the backgrounds of the key people in your organization?
   c. Do you treat them as partners and not just hired hands?
   d. Do you stay with them as a trainer until they can competently go on their own?
   e. Are they familiar with the company's vision?
   f. Have you promoted a teamwork approach where they depend on and trust each other?
   g. Did you clearly communicate your core values to your people?
4. How do you recognize your team members when they excel?
5. How do your create a sense of ownership with team members, so that when a problem surfaces they "see it, own it, solve it, do it"?

Chapter 4: Developing Your Team's Unique Talents

1. Make a list of the unique talents you bring to your business, your community, and the world.
2. What skills do others on the team have that are better than yours?
3. What is your *It*?
4. Do you manage your time, or does your time manage you? What are three things you need to do to become more effective in managing your time?

5. Do you have a plan to achieve your goals? If not, why? If so, what are your plan's key components?
6. What do you do to ensure you lead with integrity at all times?

Chapter 5: Targeting the Most Critical Information

1. Ask each member of your team to describe exactly what the team as a whole is to produce and what they personally are responsible to produce.
2. In what ways do you communicate to the members (the *Who*) on your team that you value them as individuals and care about what they think?
3. Do you know their *Whats*: their personal and professional goals, their work and personal concerns, their aspirations, their ideas on how to improve the work methods, the assignments they'd really love to have, the training they'd like to attend, etc.?
4. Look at the *Hows* your team uses to produce its results.
   a. How much do you know about each of the *Hows* (methods, processes, equipment) your team uses to produce its results?
   b. How often do you review the effectiveness and efficiency of the *Hows*?
   c. How do you determine which new *Hows* would be useful for your team to adopt?

Chapter 6: Cultivating the X Factor

1. X factor 1: The Ability to Match People and Jobs. How do you determine which people to assign to which jobs?
2. Once you have the right people in the right jobs, what do you do next to help them succeed?

3. How do you identify which of your people might need some extra help?
   a. When you identify them, how do you prepare your mentoring plan?
   b. If it appears a person needs to be replaced, what other options do you consider?
4. X factor 2: The Ability to Remove the Fog. How do you ensure all your people know the results they are expected to produce? How—and how often—do you check to verify your expectations are clearly known and are being carried out?
5. X factor 3: The Ability to Inspire and Go Higher. How do you meaningfully acknowledge your team as a whole and members individually?
6. X factor 4: The Ability to Be Creative. What plans do you have to increase the probability that opportunities will be noticed and acted on?

Chapter 7: Maintaining an Ethical Environment

1. What does skewing mean? Are you or the members of your team under its influence?
2. The phrase "breathing your own exhaust" represents how sometimes leaders gradually begin to fall in love with systems and strategies that they personally created. Can you give an example of how you have seen this happen in your own leadership?
3. What is the value that each member of your team contributes to the organization? Who are your high performers, and who is holding the team back? What are you going to do to address the issue of underperformance?
4. The way leaders respond to crises often determines their success. What are some principles of crisis management every leader needs to have in his or her arsenal?

5. When it comes to managing your people, do you lean more toward a micro- or macromanagement style? If you answered micromanaging, what can you do to build the kind of relationship with your employees that will stop you from meddling in things you need to delegate?

6. What backup plans do you have in place for when the inevitable crisis occurs?

Chapter 8: Fostering Positive Interactions

1. Trust is hard to gain and easy to lose. What are some ways leaders can gain the trust of their team members? What are some ways a leader can forfeit trust?

2. Do you feel secure enough as a leader to encourage others to challenge your systems, strategies, and opinions? Give an example of when you have done this.

3. What are you doing to integrate the different cultures, perspectives, and values of your team members into a coordinated unit? Why is time such a valuable asset when it comes to building trust within a team?

4. What are some of the most effective ways to rebuild trust when relationships within your team break down?

5. Dealing with people problems is part of the job for every leader. What are some of the most effective ways you've found to deal with such matters?

6. Do you have some team members forming subgroups or cliques? If so, what plans will you implement to build a cohesive and unified team and not allow a disjointed and dysfunctional group to dominate the culture?

Chapter 9: Moving Forward

1. If you want to accomplish something great, then you must do something. What have you done lately that will move you farther down the road to greatness?
2. Describe the differences between someone who is a workhorse, and someone who is a show horse. Which are you, and why? How would others describe you?
3. We all have areas where we're not strong. What are yours? What are you doing to address them?
4. Why do you think so few people are grinders when it comes to work? What are some ways leaders can encourage their team members to become grinders?
5. Explain how you could use the Good, the Bad, and the Ugly performance review in your organization.

Chapter 10: Prepare for Places Unexpected

1. The statement "Be slow to speak and quick to listen" is easier said than done. What are some things leaders can do to become better listeners? Who are the best listeners you know, and exactly what makes them that way?
2. How do you build strong connections with the members of your team? What can you do to further strengthen those relationships and build new ones?
3. Do you find it easier to catch people doing something right or catch them making mistakes? How can you guard against a negative mindset going forward?
4. Management by walking around is a powerful leadership technique. What does it mean to you, and how can you improve the ways in which you use it in your organization?

5. How often, and in what ways, do you currently provide feedback to the members of your team? What can you do, starting today, to improve your feedback process?

Chapter 11: Signed, Sealed, and Delivered

1. How can you build on your company's past while charting a course for its future?
2. Why is it important to build your organization around team players, not superstars?
3. How can you build a more adaptable organization?
4. In what ways do you put your customer first?
5. What reminders do you put in place to keep your humility in check?

And finally . . .

What is your biggest takeaway from reading this book, and what is one way it has changed you as a leader?

Endnotes

1. http://www.ups.com/content/us/en/about/facts/worldwide.html.

2. *Our Partnership Legacy—Jim Casey*, UPS (1991), p. 9.

3. *Our Partnership Legacy—Jim Casey*, UPS (1991), p. 13.

4. *Our Partnership Legacy—Jim Casey*, UPS (1991) p. 38.

5. *Our Partnership Legacy—Jim Casey*, UPS (1991), p. 38.

6. *Our Partnership Legacy—Jim Casey*, UPS (1991), p. 27.

7. http://www.nytimes.com/2015/07/07/sports/soccer/womens-world-cup
-final-was-most-watched-soccer-game-in-united-states-history.html?_r=0

8. Amy Alexander, "UPS Founder Jim Casey Delivered Goods the Best,"
Investor's Business Daily, http://repubhub.icopyright.net/freePost.act?tag
=3.8218?icx_id=674589.

9. Randy Gravitt, "Gaps," http://randygravitt.com/gaps/.

10. "John F. Kennedy and PT-109," *John F. Kennedy Presidential Library and
Museum*, http://www.jfklibrary.org/JFK/JFK-in-History/John-F-Kennedy
-and-PT109.aspx.

11. *Our Partnership Legacy—Jim Casey*, UPS (1991), p. 7.

The "We" (It's Not Just Me!)

This book has been a group effort, and I want to thank my four core team members.

James Fallon

A lifelong student of leadership, Jim is corporate client group director and senior vice president for a global financial services firm. For the past nineteen years, Jim has been an active member of the Real Deal, a leadership study group comprised prominent leaders from both the corporate and nonprofit worlds. Jim and I are partners in the Number One Group, which produces media content in the publishing, music, and television/film industries. You can connect with Jim at james.fallon@icloud.com.

Randy Gravitt

Randy is a writer, speaker, and life coach who coauthored *Finding Your Way*. Randy has spoken in the United States, Asia, Africa, and South America. Thousands of people each day read his blog. Randy is available to speak to organizations of all sizes on the principles in *Leadership Lessons from a UPS Driver*. You can connect with Randy through his website, RandyGravitt.com, or via Twitter @randygravitt.

Gary Mastro

Gary is responsible for the sales of *Leadership Lessons from a UPS Driver.* Gary is a thirty-eight-year veteran of UPS, where he was corporate vice president of brand and product marketing.

David Schiff

For more than thirty years, as the founder of The Operant Group, Inc., David has led project teams and taught human performance engineering to Fortune 500 companies and other prominent organizations. He also works with the military, law enforcement, and other governmental agencies to provide performance-based training to their staff instructors and internal consultants. He has published numerous articles and authored the *Consultant's Digest.*

Acknowledgments

Peter Economy helped us organize and tighten up the final manuscript. It was Peter who brought it all together and in the end was responsible for connecting us with our fine partners at Berrett-Koehler Publishing.

A heartfelt thanks goes to Leslie Stephen for her vernacular and structural engineering of the manuscript. Because of her patience and advice, and more hours of rewrites than can be counted, we were able to stay on track and pull out the best of our thoughts and experiences.

Cregg McKinney spent countless hours helping with our project. Cregg, along with Senator John Albers, is represented by the Number One Group, who is producing a movie based on a book they wrote called *The Entitled Soul*.

We appreciate the work of Mike McAlpine, Michael Agrippina, Roger Bonds, Mike Briggs, Edna Dawson, Matt Kunz, Bob and Linda Meyers, David Murray, John Quattrocchi, Jenny and Benjamin Schiff, and Kate Wallace.

Much gratitude goes out to Bob, Mark, and Jan Babcock and Laura Lyn Donahue, who helped shape the initial draft. Thanks to Stephanie Wetzel for her invaluable advice.

I'd also like to thank Nancy Baeur for her special touch during the final phase of our editing process. Great thanks to my pastor and friend, Steven Gibbs. Steven is the pastor of Stonecreek Church in Milton, Georgia. Stonecreek has a drive to do great things and mobilizes people to create lasting change in the world.

Index

About the Author

Ron Wallace is the former president of UPS International, where he was responsible for UPS in more than 200 countries and territories and had more than 60,000 people under his direction. He also served on the corporate management committee that oversaw the day-to-day operations of UPS and its 435,000 employees. In addition, he served as chairman or cochairman of 33 boards of directors of highly successful companies around the world.

Shortly after retiring from UPS, Ron was appointed by the governor of Georgia as chairman of the governor's commission and was charged with forming the city of Milton, Georgia. In 2008, Ron and a friend established the famous Olde Blind Dog Irish Pub in Milton. In 2015, it was named the best Irish pub in the world, making it the first pub in the United States to win the award. In his earlier days, Ron was a professional race car driver and later played semipro American football in Europe. He has been in law enforcement for more than twelve years since retiring from UPS. He is currently a police officer near his hometown as well as a director on several boards, political advisory committees, and charitable foundations.

In addition to overseeing several businesses and real estate developments that he owns, Ron is a campaign consultant and author of the book *Power of the Campaign Pyramid*. In 2014, he and Bob Meyers published a 336-page coffee-table book titled *Irish Pubs in America: History, Lore, and Recipes*. It won the prestigious Indie Book Award. Portions of the book are being made into a TV series, for which Ron serves as executive producer.

Ron and his wife, Kate, are blessed to have their daughter Lara, and her husband, David, along with their grandchildren, Kelly and Megan, living close to them.

Visit our website at www.leadershiplessonsbyronwallace .com/ups. Watch for the release of Ron's next book, based on his experience as a ranch hand, titled *Leadership Lessons from the Old West*.

Berrett–Koehler
Publishers

Connecting people and ideas
to create a world that works for all

Dear Reader,

Thank you for picking up this book and joining our worldwide community of Berrett-Koehler readers. We share ideas that bring positive change into people's lives, organizations, and society.

To welcome you, we'd like to offer you a free e-book. You can pick from among twelve of our bestselling books by entering the promotional code **BKP92E** here: http://www.bkconnection.com/welcome.

When you claim your free e-book, we'll also send you a copy of our e-news-letter, the *BK Communiqué*. Although you're free to unsubscribe, there are many benefits to sticking around. In every issue of our newsletter you'll find

- A free e-book
- Tips from famous authors
- Discounts on spotlight titles
- Hilarious insider publishing news
- A chance to win a prize for answering a riddle

Best of all, our readers tell us, "Your newsletter is the only one I actually read." So claim your gift today, and please stay in touch!

Sincerely,

Charlotte Ashlock
Steward of the BK Website

Questions? Comments? Contact me at bkcommunity@bkpub.com.

Certified

Corporation
bcorporation.net